READY TO LEARN

Ready to Learn

A MANDATE FOR THE NATION

ERNEST L. BOYER

THE CARNEGIE FOUNDATION
FOR THE ADVANCEMENT OF TEACHING

5 IVY LANE, PRINCETON, NEW JERSEY 08540

Library of Congress Cataloging-in-Publication Data

Carnegie Foundation for the Advancement of Teaching.
   Ready to learn : a mandate for the nation.
     p. cm. — (A Special report)
   Includes bibliographical references and index.
   ISBN 0-931050-44-8
   1. Readiness for school—United States. 2. Early childhood education—United States.
3. Child development—United States. 4. Education—United States—Aims and objectives.
5. Education and state—United States. 6. Educational surveys—United States.
I. Title. II. Series: Special report (Carnegie Foundation for the Advancement of Teaching)
LB1132.C374   1991   91-46817
372.21′0973—dc20   CIP

Second printing, 1992

Copies are available from the
PRINCETON UNIVERSITY PRESS
3175 Princeton Pike
Lawrenceville, New Jersey 08648

Contents

ACKNOWLEDGMENTS

I AM ALWAYS STRUCK, at the end of a project, by how many people contributed their time, energy, and intellect to reach the goal. But this study, particularly, involved the hard work of many colleagues and friends and proved to be, for everyone, a labor not only of professional commitment but of love and concern for children.

Everyone involved in the project credits first of all the John D. and Catherine T. MacArthur Foundation for recognizing early on the importance of this study and providing a generous grant to help support the work. John Corbally, former president, and Adele Simmons, current president, maintained active interest throughout. In addition, we thank Peter Gerber of the MacArthur Foundation for his deep commitment. Because of the funding and continuing encouragement by these colleagues, the project was sustained. We also thank the Phillips Petroleum Foundation for their grant, which helped support the study in its earliest stages.

The Board of Trustees of The Carnegie Foundation must be recognized here for their commitment to the study. *Ready to Learn* explores issues outside the traditional areas of Foundation work, but the trustees had a clear vision of its timeliness and its relevance to educational excellence.

Every single member of the staff contributed in some way to the study. I must thank, most especially, Sally Reed and Robert Hochstein. They worked nights and weekends to keep the project moving forward, and *Ready to Learn* simply would not have been completed now without their extraordinarily dedicated commitment, professional contributions, and personal sacrifice. Sally continuously managed the organizational pieces, directing the work of others while also researching and drafting parts of the report and completing the citation work. Bob's wise counsel and support have seen me through many projects over the years, and on this study his presence here and his professional contributions were particularly crucial.

Special mention must also be made of the researchers and writers whose work helped shape the manuscript. These people researched the scholarship on children's issues, surveyed the broad range of activity taking place today to improve children's lives, and drafted papers and edited text for the report. Dale Coye's work, during every phase, contributed important ideas and created a foundation on which other researchers could build. Mary Huber's clear analysis and organization helped steer the project over time. Vito Perrone steadily provided his knowledge of education and his commitment to children, and Gene Maeroff contributed his valuable field research and writing. Mary Ellen Bafumo, Jan Hempel, and Lynn Jenkins joined the project later and helped carry the research and writing through the final stages. Jan was also responsible for readying the manuscript for production and seeing the project through to bound books. Hinda Greenberg, director of the Foundation's Information Center, gave crucial support for all research activity.

Several people joined the research staff especially for this project and wrote excellent papers which contributed greatly to our study: David Greenberg, Amy Hillier, and Jack Osander. Jack also stayed on to assist with the bibliographical work. Alan Stone, writer, lawyer, and former staff director of the U.S. House Committee on Children, Youth and Families, provided extensive research, particularly on children's health issues.

Warren Bryan Martin and Ernest Boyer, Jr., also read drafts and offered valuable advice clearly informed by their concern for children, and I thank them for their contributions.

For the Foundation's National Survey of Kindergarten Teachers and the Survey of Fifth- and Eighth-Graders, which contributed so much to the outcome of the study, I thank J. Eugene Haas, Mary Jean Whitelaw, and Lois Harwood.

I must give a particularly huge and heartfelt thanks to the Foundation's word processing staff: Dee Sanders, director, Dawn Ott, Laura Bell, and Kelli-ann Korin Lanino. There is no conceivable way the project could have been accomplished as it was without their endless patience, good spirit, and tireless efforts.

Louise Underwood provided a constant source of encouragement along with invaluable, day-to-day, practical support. David Walter provided on-going technical support. Jeanine Natriello worked tirelessly on the press mailing, assisted with publicity work, and helped answer the countless calls coming in about the report. Arlene Hobson-Gundrum also helped with mailings, and Jacquelyn Minning fielded phone calls. Carol Lasala provided secretarial assistance, along with Audrey Allen. Pat Klensch-Balmer assisted in the library. Robert Lucas also worked on the huge mailing that accompanied the release. Judy Williams helped in our Washington office.

I deeply appreciate all of these staff members and thank them for their enthusiastic support.

This study depended on many other people as well. Background research and papers, or editorial work, were also contributed by: Anne Bridgman, Ingrid Canright Morgan, Betty Watts Carrington, Ann Cook, Virginia B. Edwards, Sara Hanhan, David Twenhafel, and Mark Whitaker. Also Bret Birdsong, John E. Gallagher, Lauren Maidment Green, R. Craig Sautter, and Jennifer Stoffel.

We recognize and thank these advisors on the project: David Elkind, professor, Tufts University, Elliot-Pearson Department of Child Study; Howard Gardner, professor and co-director of Project Zero, Harvard University; David Hornbeck, former superintendent of schools, Maryland State Department of Education and trustee of The Carnegie Foundation, now education advisor for the National Center on Education and the Economy and the Business Roundtable; Greg Humphrey, director of legislation, American Federation of Teachers; Lilian Katz, director, ERIC Clearinghouse on Elementary and Early Childhood Education; and Catherine Loughlin, professor of elementary education, University of New Mexico.

Also, G. Niobe Marshall, former public policy analyst, National Black Child Development Institute; Deborah Meier, director, Central Park

East Secondary School, New York; Myriam Met, foreign language coordinator, Montgomery County Schools; Aurelio Montemayor, former chairperson of the board, National Coalition of Advocates for Students; Donald Moore, director, Designs for Change, Chicago Schoolwatch; Ann Rosewater, former staff director, House Select Committee on Children, Youth, and Families; and Samuel Sava, executive director, National Association of Elementary School Principals.

We thank also Helen Blank, senior program associate, Child-Care Division, Children's Defense Fund; Gilson Brown, former executive director, Association for Childhood Education International; Bettye Caldwell, Donaghey Distinguished Professor of Education, University of Arkansas at Little Rock; Bea Cameron, associate superintendent, Student Services and Special Education, Fairfax County Schools; Robert Chase, vice-president, National Education Association; Ted Chittenden, senior research scientist, Educational Testing Service; Constance Clayton, superintendent of schools for the School District of Philadelphia; Hubert Dyasi, director, Workshop Center, City College, New York.

We thank the following people who did field research such as visits to preschools and interviews with parents: Maja Apelman, Mary E. Baldwin, Ingrid Canright Morgan, William R. Fielder, Helen LaMar, Catherine E. Loughlin, Charlayne Myers, Pearl M. Rosenberg, Lauren Sosniak, Elsa K. Weber.

Earlier survey work was conducted by Lane Mann and the Wirthlin Group of McLean, Virginia. The Wirthlin Group conducted the more recent survey of kindergarten teachers as well.

We wish to thank the following people for their help to the Foundation in a preliminary survey of kindergarten teachers: Jackie Ancess, New York City Public Schools; Richard Benjamin, superintendent, Ann Arbor, Michigan, Public Schools; Pat Bolaños, principal, Key School, Indianapolis, Indiana; Hubert Dyasi, City College of New York; Andrew Edwards, Georgia Southern University; Bena Kallick, Westport, Connecticut; Glenn Melvey, Fargo, North Dakota Public Schools; Don Monroe, superintendent, Winnetka Public Schools; Charlayne Myers,

Minneapolis Public Schools; Nancy Parachini, elementary school principal, Los Angeles Unified School District; Joseph Petner, principal, Haggerty Elementary School, Cambridge Public Schools; Nancy Place, Bellevue, Washington Public Schools; Jean Stevenson, Rosary College, Oak Park, Illinois; Takako Suzuki, administrator, Los Angeles Unified School District; Richard Van Dongen, University of New Mexico.

We offer a special thanks to all the teachers throughout the nation who kindly took the time to respond to our surveys.

The Foundation wishes also to thank Carol Jeffery and all the skilled craftspeople at the Princeton University Press for producing the bound books under a tight deadline. We also gratefully acknowledge Patricia Marks for her assistance in the final weeks with copyediting and indexing the report.

Once again, my wife, Kay, has been the inspiration that made it possible for this book to be completed. Not only did she accept graciously the endless hours involved in drafting and editing the manuscript, but more important, she contributed to its content, commenting wisely on both ideas and style. I am grateful beyond words for her support.

ERNEST L. BOYER

President
The Carnegie Foundation
for the Advancement of Teaching

TWO OF MY GRANDCHILDREN are still in their preschool years. Three-year-old Julie lives in Princeton, New Jersey. She loves to visit the public library, look at books with her father, sing along with a tape recorder, take walks with her mother, and spend lots of time romping with her older brother and sisters. When Julie was born she was held and hugged in the first moments of life by her parents, sisters, brother, and grandparents.

Meanwhile David, also three, lives two thousand miles away in Blue Creek Village, Belize. He chats away in three languages (English, Mayan, and Ketchi), plays with siblings, looks at books with his father and mother, takes care of animals, chases after birds, and runs free along the river. The first time I made the journey to see David, he was but one day old, and I was reminded again just how much young children have in common, how they all have such wonderful potential, and how they teach us universal truths.

Julie and David are growing up in very different worlds. No one knows the future. At present, their prospects appear bright, but I often reflect on the kind of world they will inherit. And I think, as well, about the other nineteen million preschoolers here in the United States, some of whom are struggling against great odds, facing debilitating experiences that may diminish their capacity to grow and learn.

This report, *Ready to Learn,* is about our nation's children, and how we can be sure that all of them are ready for school. Its origins go back to the mid-eighties. At that time, The Carnegie Foundation for the Advancement of Teaching had just released two policy reports, one on high school, the other on college. We were participating actively in what's become known as ''the school reform movement.''

Going from place to place, I was struck that many schools in this country are truly outstanding. Others range from good to mediocre, functioning with mixed results. I was also concerned that the most troubled schools were frequently overlooked, leaving many of the root causes of our educational problems unexamined. I was impressed, as well, that much of the focus of reform was on secondary schools, failing to acknowledge the importance of early education. Thus, I came to believe that we needed to step back and look at very young children, and consider the context in which they are coming of age to begin formal schooling.

It was against this backdrop then that we launched a study called "The Early Years." We visited schools, interviewed teachers, met with parents, and conducted surveys. We concluded, from this preliminary work, that vast numbers of children are at risk, not just the poor. And we began to prepare a special report that combined our findings about preschool and primary education.

Midway through this project, President Bush called the nation's governors to Charlottesville, Virginia, for an education summit. This was soon followed by a historic announcement by the President—six goals for the nation's schools. I was impressed by all of the goals, but the first one was most compelling. By the year 2000, the President proclaimed, all children will come to school "ready to learn." Just what would it take, we wondered, to ensure that every child in the country would, in fact, be well prepared for school?

Another development gave focus to our study. About one year ago, I was asked to work with the National Education Goals Panel, ably chaired by Governor Roy Romer of Colorado, to determine ways to measure the nation's first education goal. We found that, at present, there are no "direct" ways to assess the school readiness of children. We did, however, look at "indirect" measures, such as the prenatal care of mothers, the birthweight of babies, and preschool education. We concluded that many children are at risk of failure before they come to school. It seemed inappropriate to focus on measuring outcomes without giving equal attention to improving children's prospects for success in school.

In commenting on the influences that shaped this report, I should also mention teachers. During school visits and in response to our surveys, teachers spoke to us movingly about how troubled and anxious children are and how life outside the school relates to learning. They noted, too, that children increasingly are coming to school with language deficiencies that diminish their capacity to succeed.

Also my wife, Kay, had an important role to play. For nearly forty years, she has worked clinically with mothers and babies. Her experience has profoundly shaped my thinking about early education, helping to convince me that what happens to children before school—even before birth itself—will influence their performance, and that good nutrition, a safe and healthy birth, and emotional bonding are vital. In short, I've been taught that health and education are inseparably related.

With these thoughts in mind, I became persuaded that school reformers have not yet gotten to the heart of the matter. Surely we need structural changes in schools and more effective models for the future. But what about today? Family life has weakened. Children are at risk. Neighborhoods are less supportive. It seems clear that we cannot have islands of academic excellence in a sea of community indifference. If we truly hope to improve education, we must begin to focus immediately and decisively on children.

During the past months, as people learned that we were preparing a report on "school readiness," they acknowledged that it was critically important, agreeing that all children should come to school well prepared. But at least occasionally, we also heard that the first education goal is far too idealistic. "We have neither the resources nor the will to prepare all children for school," is the way one critic put it. Perhaps. But I'm still convinced that the President and governors got it right. The quality of education, and of our society, *will* be measured by our capacity to care for our children and to make sacrifices for their future.

There is, of course, an equally urgent obligation to make certain that schools are prepared for children. We dare not develop arbitrary hurdles for school admission that label children, sort them, or screen them out because they don't fit a certain mold. Schools surely need to receive every child, offering creative programs. And The Carnegie Foundation is, even now, working on a follow-up study on primary education. Still, the need to consider what is happening to children *before* school cannot be denied.

What follows, then, in this report, *Ready to Learn,* is a blueprint for action, one that all Americans, acting together, might follow on behalf of children. We have sought to identify ways to support families, providing for them a more caring, more compassionate network of support. Above all, the focus is on children, since *Ready to Learn* is, in the end, about ensuring that all youngsters are well prepared, not just for schooling but for life.

READINESS FOR ALL

READINESS FOR ALL

AMERICA IS LOSING SIGHT of its children. In decisions made every day we are placing them at the very bottom of the agenda, with grave consequences for the future of the nation. It's simply intolerable that millions of children in this country are physically and emotionally disadvantaged in ways that restrict their capacity to learn, especially when we know what a terrible price will be paid for such neglect, not just educationally, but in tragic human terms as well.

For nearly a decade now, school renewal has been high on the national agenda. Graduation requirements have been tightened. Teaching standards have been raised, and student assessment has become a major priority for education. In recent years, a host of bold innovations—"teacher empowerment," "school-based management," "parental choice," "new schools for a new century"—have been proposed in quick succession. Most consequentially, perhaps, governors and corporate leaders have become vigorous advocates of school reform.

The quality of our schools and the nation's future are inseparably connected. For America to be secure, quality education is required and excellence for every student must be vigorously reaffirmed. People who cannot communicate are powerless. People who know nothing of their past are culturally impoverished. People who are poorly trained are ill-prepared to face the future. Without good schools, America cannot remain civically vital or economically competitive, and educational reform, unquestionably, must be aggressively pursued.

But in our search for excellence, *children* have somehow been forgotten. We have ignored the fundamental fact that to improve the nation's schools, a solid foundation must be laid. We have failed to recognize that the family may be a more imperiled institution than the school and

3

that many of education's failures relate to problems that precede schooling, even birth itself. We have focused on school outcomes, forgetting that if children do not have a good beginning—if they are not well nurtured and well loved during the first years of life—it will be difficult, if not impossible, to compensate fully for such failings later on.

The harsh truth is that in America today vast numbers of our children are growing up without good health care, without supportive families, and without the love they need to become successful, independent learners. Schools, in turn, are being asked to do what homes and churches and communities have not been able to accomplish, and if teachers fail anywhere along the line, we condemn them for not meeting our high-minded expectations.

There is no evidence that today's parents are any less committed or less caring. As much as any previous generation, they're deeply concerned about the well-being of their children and worry in the dark of night about how to make them happy and secure. What *has* changed, however, is the loss of community, the increased fragmentation of family life, the competing, often conflicting, pressures that keep family members on the go and out of touch with one another. Time seems so limited, schedules so hectic, and in many households, parents—who often lack support—feel torn between work and family obligations. In such a climate, children suffer most.

Beyond all this are the painful pathologies experienced by children who are least advantaged. Poor children are more likely to be physically handicapped, more likely to be language deficient, more likely to be victims of violence, and more likely to be damaged by drug abuse. Yet, it is an unspeakable disgrace that, here in the United States, one in every four children under the age of six is growing up in a family that cannot afford safe housing, good nutrition, or quality health care—conditions that should be the right of *every* child.

During the second week of school, at a hurried twenty-minute lunch break, a veteran kindergarten teacher gave us these impressions: "The year is off to a good start," she said, "but I worry about what's going on outside the school, in neighborhoods, and homes. I've noticed in the

4

last few years that children's lives are not running smoothly. A lot of them seem anxious. I have kids who come to school hungry. I know that sometimes they're abused. They don't get the strong support they need at home, and frankly, I really fear for the future of these children—and their families.''[1]

Thus, one point is clear: In our search for excellence in education, children must come first. Policymakers simply must look beyond the schoolhouse door and consider what is happening to childhood itself. The time has come to recognize that what children need is not just ''more assessment'' but more compassion and support, that what we must offer them is not just a ''restructured school'' but assurance that they belong. While focusing on outcomes, reformers must be equally concerned about preparing children for schooling in the first place.

The good news is that national priorities may be shifting. In his first State of the Union Message, President George Bush, in an unprecedented move, announced six ambitious goals for all the nation's schools—mandates quickly adopted by governors from the fifty states. By the year 2000, he declared, every child in America should start school ready to learn, school dropouts should decline, and our education system should become world-class in math and science. All schools, the President declared, should be disciplined and drug free, students should be tested in core subjects, and within a decade America should achieve literacy for all adults.

Every one of these goals is consequential. Each should be vigorously pursued. But it is the President's *first* goal that stands out far above all the rest. To say that, within a decade, every single child in America will come to school ''ready to learn'' is a bold, hugely optimistic proposition. Still, dreams can be fulfilled only when they've been defined, and if we as a nation can ensure that every child is well prepared for school, it seems reasonable to expect that all the other education goals will, in large measure, be achieved.

The focus of our concern must be *children*—not just the schools. Indeed, what is so encouraging about the nation's first education goal—the part we find so compelling—is that the school-reform movement,

5

which for years has been searching for the right *ending,* suddenly has been given a challenging new *beginning*.

While we get all children ready for school, we must, of course, get schools ready for children—ready to accept with hope and enthusiasm every child who comes to the schoolhouse door. Children are, after all, always learning. "The child is the most avid learner of all living things on this earth," is the way Ashley Montagu put it.[2] From the moment of birth, youngsters begin exploring their world, extending their horizons. It's in the early years when children discover windows to the vast world that lies before them. And so, when we speak of "ready to learn," what we really mean is successfully preparing all children for school.

But we have a very long way to go. Today, far too many of the nation's children come to school without a good beginning. They are shockingly restricted in their potential for learning even before their first formal lesson, "destined for school failure because of poverty, neglect, sickness, handicapping conditions, and lack of adult protection and nurturance," according to educational researcher Harold Hodgkinson.[3]

In another sobering assessment, the Southern Regional Education Board, after evaluating the school readiness of children in that part of the country, concluded: "Today not all children are ready to begin the first grade. Too many never catch up. Unless additional steps are taken, possibly one-third of the approximately one million children projected to be entering the first grade will not be ready to do so in the year 2000."[4]

In the summer of 1991, The Carnegie Foundation for the Advancement of Teaching surveyed more than seven thousand kindergarten teachers to learn about the readiness of children. Teachers were, it seemed to us, an important point of reference. After all, they are with youngsters every day, watching their reactions, observing their relationships with others, noting their struggles and successes. Teachers, especially the sensitive, seasoned ones, have a keen, almost intuitive, understanding of children's needs.

Therefore, we asked kindergarten teachers how well prepared their students are for formal education, focusing especially on physical

6

Figure 1

How Does the Readiness of Your Students Today
Compare to Five Years Ago?

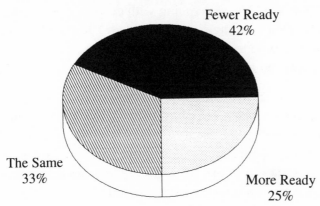

Fewer Ready
42%

The Same
33%

More Ready
25%

SOURCE: The Carnegie Foundation for the Advancement of Teaching, National Survey of Kindergarten
Teachers, 1991.

well-being, social confidence, emotional maturity, language richness, general knowledge, and moral awareness—what we define as the key dimensions of school readiness.

Frankly, we found it deeply troubling, ominous really, that 35 percent of the nation's children—more than one in three—are *not* ready for school, according to the teachers. Even more disturbing, when we asked how the readiness of last year's students compared to those who enrolled five years ago, 42 percent of the respondents said the situation is getting *worse;* only 25 percent said it's better (figure 1). When asked to identify the areas in which students are most deficient, teachers overwhelmingly cited "lack of proficiency in language." In response to the question "What would most improve the school readiness of children?" the majority said, "Parent education."[5]

Almost all teachers also took time to write revealing, often poignant comments about their students. One observed: "It is so sad to realize just how many children are not ready to learn when they come to school. They deserve to know by age five their full name and the name of the town where they live. They need to know that a pencil is some-

7

thing they write with—not eat—and that someone believes in them, no matter what!'' Another teacher wrote: ''Too many of my children come to school hungry. They are tired or in need of much love and attention. More and more students are coming with deep emotional problems that interfere with their learning.'' A third added: ''It's terribly discouraging to see children come to school who don't know where they live, can't identify colors, and are unable to recite their full and proper name.''

How can this nation live comfortably with the fact that so many of our children experience such crippling deprivations? How can we ignore the conditions that place them at such disadvantage and make their prospect for successful schooling doubtful? Surely, America has within its power the means to make the earliest years, for all children, enriching and productive. But do we have the will?

Kristin Sonquist, a kindergarten teacher in Minneapolis and a mother of four, wrote this note at the bottom of our questionnaire: ''Children need to be healthy in mind, soul, and body to be ready to learn. They need more laptime with their parents so they know they are loved. They need to know, for sure, that there will be a roof over their heads and food on the table tomorrow. Here in Minnesota, they need mittens and boots in the winter. These things should be basic rights,'' she added, ''but today they are *not* guaranteed to all children.''

Whose responsibility is it to assure the school readiness of children? Who should take the lead in seeing to it that *every* child receives not just food, protection, and love, but also the guidance and the richness of experience needed to succeed in school and proceed, with confidence, in life?

We begin, where we must, with parents. When all is said and done, mothers and fathers are the first and most essential teachers. It's in the home that children must be clothed, fed, and loved. This is the place where life's most basic lessons will be learned. And no outside program—no surrogate or substitute arrangement—however well planned or well intended, can replace a supportive family that gives the child emotional security and a rich environment for learning.

8

Still, parents cannot do the job alone. It is simply unrealistic to expect mothers and fathers, acting on their own, to be heroically self-sufficient. Yet, here in America, the family is so often portrayed as carrying on in splendid isolation, solving every crisis in quick, thirty-minute segments, as in the popular television sitcoms "Leave It to Beaver," "The Brady Bunch," or "Father Knows Best."

But that's just not the way it works. While cherishing their privacy and freedom, parents have always looked to others for support. In less mobile, more insular times, children were born at home with neighbors and midwives in attendance. Family doctors made house calls. Grandparents, aunts, uncles, and cousins often stopped by for casual conversation. Neighbors watched over kids, patching up cuts and bruises. The corner grocer kept an eye out for trouble. Pastors, priests, and rabbis ministered at times of joy and grief.

This loosely organized network of support—spreading outward from the extended family—was quite informal, even unreliable at times. Yet, when parents were anxious or confused, it was reassuring to have a wide circle of support.

Gradually, the protective ring eroded. New work patterns and increased mobility uprooted small-town life. Relatives moved away. Families became isolated, disconnected, struggling alone. Neighbors became strangers, doors were bolted, and friendliness was replaced by fear. A climate of anonymity blanketed communities. Children were warned to avoid people they didn't know, and "reaching out to touch someone" came to mean pushing electronic buttons. Modern life, which offered more conveniences and more options, destabilized former certainties and weakened traditional networks of support.

Family members still lean on one another, especially in times of crisis. But in today's fragmented, less supportive world, they increasingly must turn to outside agencies for help—to organizations that are less reliable, less caring, and certainly less knowledgeable about the child whose very survival is at stake. Parents find themselves competing on unequal terms with impersonal institutions that not only play a much bigger role in family life, but even have begun to shape it.

In many households, child-care providers, counselors, social workers, even television personalities are as influential in the lives of children as are parents who, while feeling deeply the responsibility of child rearing, have become more vulnerable and less empowered. Sociologist Kenneth Keniston describes the contemporary parent as "a coordinator without voice or authority, a maestro trying to conduct an orchestra of players who have never met. . . ."[6]

Clearly, when it comes to helping children, a balance must be struck. No one imagines returning to yesterday's more intimate communal life, or creating a romanticized version of the isolated, self-reliant family. Nor is it realistic to assume that a flurry of new governmental initiatives can do it all. And surely it's unrealistic to expect the nation's schools, acting on their own, to bring communities together or become a surrogate for the family.

Rather, the time has come to move beyond the tired old "family versus government" debate and create a new network of support. Let's agree that while the responsibility for school readiness begins with parents, it quickly reaches beyond the family to the workplace, to neighborhoods, to state capitals, and eventually to Washington, DC. What's needed is a special blend of public and private services—a new kind of extended family that is both reliable and caring. But for this to be accomplished, we must all move beyond ourselves, recognizing that "we are in truth members of one another," as Walter Lippmann said.[7]

The nation's first education goal—readiness for all—is a mandate around which everyone can rally, a pledge America has made, not only to itself, but most especially to its children. And what is crueler than to make a promise to a child and then walk away? Children are, after all, our most precious resource, and if we as a nation cannot commit ourselves to help the coming generation, if we cannot work together compassionately to assure that every child is well prepared for school, then what *will* pull us all together?

What we need is inspired leadership, a sense of urgency, and a strategy for action. Journalist Tom Bradbury reminds us, "No one is against children. The enemy is the attitude that business as usual is enough, that doing the best we can under the circumstances is adequate, that a

10

few changes and a little more money will suffice.''[8] Helping children should be viewed as an investment, not a cost, since failure to act surely will mean far higher payments later on in remedial education, in unemployment, in crime—in wasted lives and promises unfulfilled.

Thus, what we propose in this report is a decade-long campaign on behalf of children, one in which everyone is involved and no child is left out. We call for a truly *national* effort with a coordinated, grass-roots program in every community to assure that all nineteen million preschoolers will begin school ready to learn.

What follows is our plan. In it we seek to answer seven basic questions, and in so doing, define a ready-to-learn agenda for the nation, one that reaches into every neighborhood and touches every aspect of children's lives:

- How can we ensure that all children have a healthy start?

- How can every child live in a supportive, language-rich environment, guided by empowered parents?

- How can we make available to all children quality child care that provides both love and learning?

- How can work and family life be brought together through workplace policies that support parents and give security to children?

- How can television become a creative partner in a school-readiness campaign, offering to preschoolers programming that is mind enriching?

- How can we give to every child a neighborhood for learning, with spaces and places that invite play and spark the imagination?

- How can we bring the old and young together with new intergenerational arrangements that provide a community of caring for every child?

The picture we draw on the pages that follow is, in reality, a portrait of the child's world. We focus on the influences of birth, of parents, of day-care arrangements, of the workplace, of television, of neighbors, of grandparents—all of the forces that have such a profound impact on children's lives and shape their readiness to learn. Our aim is to suggest how Americans, acting together, can ensure that, by the year 2000, all children will be ready to succeed in school.

Above all, our aim is to enrich the life of every child. Only then will America's future be secure. Author Sylvia Ann Hewlett put the challenge this way: "Throughout the ages people have striven for meaning that goes beyond the narrow scope of individual lives. . . . As we head toward the twenty-first century, we may well be ready to temper our autonomous, self-absorbed drive with a concern for others. Nothing is more worth doing than easing the pain and improving the life chances of vulnerable, blameless children."[9]

It is this conviction, this public love of children, that must motivate and sustain America's ready-to-learn campaign.

An Agenda for Action

A HEALTHY START

"IN EVERY CHILD WHO IS BORN," James Agee wrote, "under no matter what circumstances, and of no matter what parents, the potentiality of the human race is born again."[1] Last year, more than 4,200,000 babies were born in the United States, the greatest number in the last thirty years.[2] The day-to-day physical nourishment these children receive—the quality of care they get during the first months and years of life—will shape profoundly their readiness for school. If there is one right that *every* child can claim, it is the right to a healthy start.

For all children to be well prepared for school, health workers and educators must join in common cause. Failure to do so will have a devastating impact on America's future, and most especially on our children. The Business Roundtable, comprised of top corporate leaders, makes this compelling claim: "Raising our expectations for educational performance will not produce the needed improvement unless we also reduce the barriers to learning that are represented by poor student health."[3]

In response, a three-pronged strategy is proposed: first, as a long-term plan, we call for a national education program, a course of study in every school to educate tomorrow's parents about good parenting and good health. Second, we urge that the federal nutrition program for women, infants, and children—better known as WIC—be fully funded. Third, to provide access to basic health care for all mothers and babies, we call for the establishment of a national network of Ready-to-Learn Clinics, building on existing services and programs.

During the past one hundred years, child health in this country has undergone a remarkable transformation. Dreaded diseases such as typhoid fever, diphtheria, tuberculosis, and polio have been largely conquered.

15

Milk contamination, which once killed thousands of children, is now effectively controlled. Mumps and measles, which still threaten, are no longer widespread epidemics. Today, the odds of a child in the United States dying from disease or injury are one-half of what they were just forty years ago.[4]

Still, rejoicing should be muted. Despite miraculous medical advances, large numbers of babies in this country are physically deprived in ways that diminish their quality of life and restrict their capacity to learn. While no child should live a single day with pangs of hunger, it is the nation's shame that nearly half a million children are malnourished and that twelve million are hungry at some time during every month.[5] It is equally disgraceful that fetal malnutrition now affects up to 10 percent of babies born in the United States. Damage to the fetus caused by poor nourishment during the twelfth to twenty-fourth weeks of gestation—a time most critical to brain growth—cannot be reversed.[6] Ultimately, low birthweight is connected to poor school performance (figure 2).

Clearly, good health begins before birth. What the pregnant woman eats and drinks influences the child's school performance later on. A mother's caloric and protein deficiency during pregnancy, for example, can permanently impair the child's learning ability through a decrease in the number of brain neurons.[7] Fetal exposure to alcohol increases the child's risk of language deficiency and mental retardation.[8] Further, when an expectant mother takes just one dose of drugs, the fetus in the amniotic sac is bathed in drugs for days, risking physical impairment.[9] Drug use by the mother or father even *before* conception may damage a child.

Mothers who smoke during pregnancy place their child at risk for low birthweight, asthma, and growth retardation.[10] Children of smokers also tend to lag behind their peers in cognitive development and educational achievement, and they are particularly subject to hyperactivity and in-attention (figure 3). Further, the effects of smoking are cumulative, with children of heavy smokers scoring lower on verbal tests than those of lighter smokers or nonsmokers.[11] As one researcher put it: ''At no other time does the well-being of one individual so directly depend on the well-being of another.''[12]

16

Figure 2

The Relationship Between
Birthweight and School Failure

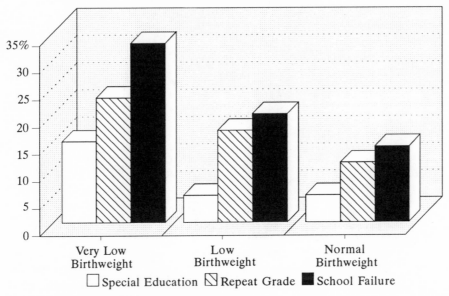

Note: Includes children ages four to seventeen.

SOURCE: Lucile Newman and Stephen L. Buka, *Every Child a Learner: Reducing Risks of Learning Impairment During Pregnancy and Infancy* (Denver: Education Commission of the States, 1990), 4.

Sadly, approximately forty thousand babies are born each year in this country with serious problems directly related to alcohol abuse by mothers during pregnancy.[13] About seven thousand of them have fetal-alcohol syndrome, a condition that results in mental retardation. Another thirty-three thousand have learning problems—limited attention span, speech and language deficiencies, and hyperactivity. Further, more than 10 percent of all newborns in the United States—425,000 in 1988—had mothers who used marijuana, cocaine, crack, heroin, or amphetamines during pregnancy. Cocaine and crack are associated with prematurity, smaller head circumference, and lower birthweight, all of which place a child educationally at risk.

Unless America takes bold steps now—unless we have dramatic intervention—this shocking pattern of child abuse is certain to continue, and

17

Figure 3

The Relationship Between Maternal Cigarette Smoking
During Pregnancy and School Failure and Learning Disability at Age Seven

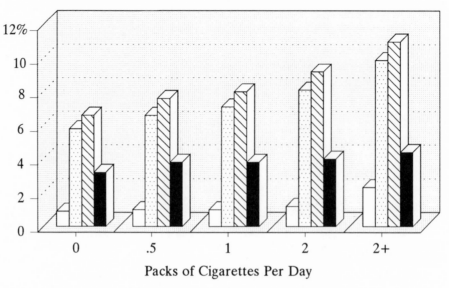

Packs of Cigarettes Per Day

☐ Special Class ▨ Repeat Grade ◹ School Failure ■ Learning Disability

SOURCE: Lucile Newman and Stephen L. Buka, *Every Child a Learner: Reducing Risks of Learning Impairment During Pregnancy and Infancy* (Denver: Education Commission of the States, 1990), 7.

perhaps increase. Consider, for example, that 91 percent of the nation's high school seniors—tomorrow's parents—already have used alcohol sometime in their lives, 66 percent have smoked cigarettes, 44 percent have tried marijuana, and 31 percent have experimented with an illicit drug other than marijuana (table 1).[14] Beyond these abuses, the nation's young people are often poorly nourished and do not get adequate exercise, factors which adversely affect their health.[15]

In a Carnegie Foundation survey of teachers, more than half of the respondents said that "poor nourishment" among students is a problem at their school. Sixty percent cited "poor health" as a problem.[16] One teacher in a midsize city observed: "Every year there seem to be more physical problems at our school that interfere with learning. I know that

18

Table 1

High School Seniors (1989) Reporting Having Tried Drugs

DRUG TYPE	PERCENTAGE
Alcohol	91%
Cigarettes	66
Marijuana/hashish	44
Illicit drugs other than marijuana	31
Cocaine	10
Crack	5

SOURCE: National Institute on Drug Abuse, 1991.

children who don't eat well or don't get rest can't do well in school. Yet, that's exactly what I'm seeing more and more." A kindergarten teacher said: "An increasing number of children who come to school have attention problems that I'm being told relate to poor nutrition and deficiencies in their diet." Another teacher told us: "Today's students take far better care of their stereos than they do their own bodies. And what's so sad is that later they'll pass on this abusive behavior to their own children."

This nation simply must interrupt the cycle of ignorance that will have such tragic consequences for the coming generation. Today's students urgently need to be taught the facts of health—as well as the facts of life. Specifically, we propose that every school district in the country offer a new health course as a requirement for graduation, with units of study threaded through the whole curriculum, from kindergarten to grade twelve. "What we need is a *national* policy," says Ramon Cortines, superintendent of schools in San Francisco, "one that supports comprehensive school health education."[17]

In our proposed curriculum—called, perhaps, "The Life Cycle"—wellness and prevention would be central integrating themes. Selected study units could be taught as separate subjects, while others might easily be woven into such courses as history, science, and physical education. Through this integrated health curriculum, students progressing from grade to grade would gain respect for their own bodies, learning to appreciate the mystery of birth, the nurturing of life, and the imperative of death. Very early, they would begin to reflect on what a truly awesome responsibility it is to bring a new life into the world.

As a capstone unit, we propose that each student participate in an "each-one-teach-one" project, passing along to family and friends what they have learned in school, thus expanding prospects for good health. There is precedent for this. At the turn of the century, a cholera epidemic swept New York City. Thousands of babies died. In response, the city's public schools organized a health course for high school girls, instructing them in the care of babies. After completing their training, the students—called "Little Mothers"—received an honor badge and became health teachers in their own homes. Each was made to understand that she had a weighty obligation to aid in saving babies' lives.[18] Could schools today introduce, for both boys and girls, a modern-day version of the student health corps that was so effectively organized nearly a century ago?

The Life Cycle curriculum we propose would vary from school to school. Still, common threads would be required. A curriculum designed by the New York Academy of Medicine illustrates what we have in mind. This health course includes a unit called "Growing Healthy" in which elementary students study physical and emotional health, family life, and the damaging effects that smoking, drugs, and alcohol have on the body. A middle-school unit called "Being Healthy" focuses on adolescent growth, physical fitness, and such issues as AIDS, "Family Living," and "Nutrition for Life."[19]

In Philadelphia, an organization called Education for Parenting has "Learning about Parenting: Learning to Care," an appealing health program for students in kindergarten to grade twelve. Students come to understand and be more cautious about becoming parents. Mothers, fathers, and their babies actually visit the classroom, giving students firsthand understanding of the challenges of raising children, allowing them to observe and record the growth and abilities of infants. For example, a young mother and her baby, Mark, visited Libby Blank's first-grade class in Pennsylvania. "Before Mark's visit," the teacher said, "we predict what he will do. We plan ways to record his actions and skills. We measure his head circumference and body length. The children then write creative stories about the baby."[20]

"Know Your Body" is a health education program developed by the American Health Foundation for students in kindergarten through grade six. It focuses on nutrition, fitness, and the prevention of smoking. In grade four, for example, students learn which sports are aerobic activities, and they study "body fuel" using food diaries and by playing "fiber detective." Two recent studies found that the program results in lower cholestorol and blood-pressure levels among students and increases their knowledge of health.[21]

Clearly, health education, when properly designed and taught, makes a difference. Even eighteen weeks of health instruction produces a significant decrease in smoking and other drug use, according to a Rand Corporation study.[22] A health education program in South Carolina was credited with reducing adolescent pregnancies. A Minnesota health project reduced the numbers of students who started smoking.[23] A Louis Harris study concluded that students in health education gained more knowledge and developed better attitudes and behavior than did students without such classes. Specifically, the percentage of students using alcohol dropped to 43 percent with one year of education, and then to 33 percent after three years of health instruction. Smoking decreased from 20 to 14 percent (table 2).[24] "The evidence is overwhelming that health education works. But *national* policy is needed," is the conclusion of the National Health/Education Consortium in Washington.[25]

Educating today's students—tomorrow's parents—is a long-term strategy, one that must begin now. Meanwhile, another crisis—poor nutrition among at-risk mothers and babies—also requires immediate attention. The reality is that if a pregnant woman does not eat well, her nutritional deficiency can interfere with the fetus's development, increasing the possibility that the baby will be malformed or mentally or physically retarded.[26] Yet, it is a disturbing fact that in the United States

Table 2

After Extended Health Education, Students Reporting That They
"Often" or "Sometimes" Use Substances

	AFTER ONE YEAR OF EDUCATION	AFTER THREE YEARS OF EDUCATION
Alcohol	43%	33%
Cigarettes	20	14
Drugs	13	6

SOURCE: The Metropolitan Life Foundation and Louis Harris and Associates, Inc., "Health You've Got to Be Taught: An Evaluation of Comprehensive Health Education in American Public Schools," 1988, 5.

today, literally hundreds of thousands of expectant mothers are under-nourished. It's unfortunate that so many mothers have not learned about the nutritional benefits of breast-feeding, and it's distressing that millions of preschool children go day after day without the nutrition needed for good health and effective learning.

How should we proceed?

The federal nutrition program called WIC was signed into law in 1972 precisely to meet the health needs of poor women, infants, and children. Milk, cheese, eggs, and cereal are distributed monthly through eight thousand service centers across the country. Currently, nearly five million low-income women and their children are being served.[27] WIC is effective. The program is successful in bringing mothers into prenatal care early, in reducing infant mortality, in raising birthweights, and later, in improving the educational performance of children. WIC is a solid economic investment, too.[28] A recent study found that every dollar invested in the program saves four dollars or more in medical costs later on.[29]

Yet, despite WIC's record of success, only 55 percent of those eligible are served, leaving millions of mothers and babies undernourished. How can we live comfortably with the fact that millions fail to receive even the minimum food supplements required for good health and successful learning? Surely the time has come to guarantee that all of the nation's mothers and babies will be well fed. We propose, therefore,

22

that WIC be fully funded—and appropriations increased from $2.4 to $4.5 billion.[30] This is a moral imperative. As Winston Churchill once said, "There is no finer investment for any community than putting milk into babies."[31]

Further, the educational component of WIC should be strengthened. According to current regulations, mothers who register for the program are eligible to receive not just good nutrition, but health instruction, too. The problem is that most WIC offices are overburdened and the teaching is often cursory at best. Still, this is a moment to be seized— an occasion when at-risk mothers can receive essential information regarding good health and child development. We propose, therefore, that every WIC office sponsor a "parent seminar series," one that covers all dimensions of school readiness, from physical well-being to moral development. The WIC appropriation should be further increased to accommodate this program.

Health education for future parents is essential. Good nutrition for poor mothers and babies is essential. A third key factor in improving the health and learning prospects of children is ensuring that all expectant mothers have quality prenatal care. The period *before* birth is critical. A healthy fetus, by the sixth month, has already developed ten billion neurons, nearly the full number needed for total brain development,[32] and if all children are to reach their full potential—if every one is to be ready to learn—pregnant mothers simply must receive good health care, beginning in the first trimester.

Infants whose mothers do *not* receive adequate care during pregnancy are more likely to be physically at-risk, intellectually deficient, and restricted in their capacity to learn.[33] Yet, one-quarter of all pregnant women in America receive belated prenatal care, or none at all.[34] Further, the percentage of women in this country getting substandard care has been growing.[35] Author Lisbeth B. Schorr, in commenting on this crisis, observed: "The United States is virtually alone among nations— and absolutely alone among Western industrial democracies—in its grudging approach to the provision of maternity care. Government in the United States has . . . never assumed responsibility for assuring that every pregnant woman gets the health care she needs to maximize the chances of a healthy birth."[36]

The most formidable barrier is cost. Medicaid, authorized by Congress in 1965, provides health coverage for more than twenty-seven million people. Yet nine million women of reproductive age have no health insurance of any kind.[37] In addition, even though Medicaid coverage has been expanded to include young children, there are still 1.5 million youngsters under the age of six not covered by this or any other program.[38] Universal health insurance is essential.

But even with full coverage, millions of women and children still would remain unserved because of a chaotic *delivery* system, one that makes access to health care so shockingly uneven. In rural areas where 20 percent of Americans reside, hundreds of health clinics have closed in recent years.[39] For many, prenatal care is miles away, or nonexistent. In Georgia, for example, ninety-two counties have no obstetrician, forty counties have no hospital, and thirteen counties have no family physician.[40] "In many rural communities of Michigan, mothers may have to travel a hundred miles or more to get prenatal care," according to Veda Sharp of the Michigan Department of Health. Even in large cities, with sprawling medical centers and well-trained physicians, health care in the poorest neighborhoods has actually decreased in the past twenty years, leaving mothers and children with no place to go.[41] This is inexcusable.

Basic health care for mothers and their babies must become a top national priority, a position vigorously being promoted by the National Governors' Association. In their 1990 report, the governors declared: "If steps are not taken now to build a real health-care system, too many children will continue to come to school unprepared to learn, too many adolescents will continue to face serious but preventable health problems."[42] Therefore, we call for a national network of "one-stop shopping" health and education centers to serve all low-income mothers and children. These centers—which could be called Ready-to-Learn Clinics—would integrate health, education, and social services, building on the current system and making it more equitable and more accessible.

24

Marian Wright Edelman, president of the Children's Defense Fund, powerfully states the challenge: "Children must have their basic needs for health care . . . and nutrition met if they are to be prepared to achieve in school. A child with an undiagnosed vision problem, or without the means to get glasses once a problem has been diagnosed, hardly can learn to his potential. A child whose intellectual development is stunted by lead poisoning cannot excel in the classroom. . . . Nor can a hungry child. . . . All of this is common sense. Any parent, any teacher, any doctor, any politician understands these connections. The puzzling thing is why we can't do what we all know makes sense, giving all children the essential and cost-effective early investments they need to prepare them to achieve."[43]

Creating a *national* network of Ready-to-Learn Clinics—one that builds on and extends the current, fragmented "system"—would, at first blush, appear to be a hugely complicated task. But this is something America can and must do. Let's not forget that we created, in this country, a network of public schools—eighty-three thousand of them—from Bangor, Maine, to Honolulu, Hawaii, serving forty-one million children. This was accomplished precisely because the nation's citizens shared a conviction that educating every child was far too important to be left to chance.

The time has come to create a common *health* network, modeled after the common *school*. Today, no one would tolerate a fragmented education system in which some children went off to school each morning, while others stayed home with no place to go. How, then, can we tolerate, year after year, a broken system of health care that denies access to millions of our children? After all, health is a *prerequisite* to education. Julius Richmond, the former U.S. surgeon general, states that the national movement toward school-based health care is an idea "whose time seems to have arrived. The idea is to provide services that are comprehensive."[44]

A Ready-to-Learn Clinic would offer prenatal and maternal care for mothers, as well as health services to children up to age five, including regular checkups, routine screening for hearing and vision problems,

25

Table 3

Preschool Children Who Have Completed Immunizations

	YEAR	DTP	MEASLES	POLIO
United States	1985	64.9%	60.8%	55.3%
Belgium	1987	95.0	90.0	99.0
Denmark	1987	94.0	82.0	100.0
England and Wales	1987	87.0	76.0	87.0
France	1986	97.0	55.0	97.0
Germany (FRG)	1987	95.0	50.0	95.0
The Netherlands	1987	96.9	92.8	96.9
Norway	1987	80.0	87.0	80.0
Spain	1986	88.0	83.0	80.0
Switzerland	1986	90–98	60–70	95–98

SOURCES: Combined sources; see C. Arden Miller and Bret Williams, *Preventive Health Care for Young Children: Findings from a 10-Country Study and Directions for United States Policy* (Washington, DC: 1991), 76.

and testing for lead poisoning, which the American Academy of Pediatrics recently labeled an "epidemic."[45] Protecting every child against childhood diseases through inoculation is crucial, too. Indeed, it is inexcusable that 20 percent of our preschool children have not been vaccinated against polio, that the incidence of whooping cough is three times higher than it was a decade ago, and that the reported cases of measles skyrocketed to more than twenty-six thousand in 1990.[46] Surely, this nation can accomplish something as simple, and as essential, as protecting every child against these contagious childhood illnesses (table 3).

A Ready-to-Learn Clinic would build on existing services—especially county health clinics. It would serve as an education referral center and establish a collaborative relationship with WIC. Above all, the proposed clinic would work closely with Head Start and the schools, even perhaps locating the project at or near a school since health and education are so closely tied. Further, schools are found in every neighborhood. They have wide public trust and to have a health service close by would benefit both institutions, and their clients, too. Finally, an interagency advisory body might be formed to ensure that the various health and education institutions in the county work together toward common goals.

States should take the lead in creating Ready-to-Learn Clinics, just as they have led the way in building a network of public schools. To begin the process, we propose that a county-by-county Maternal and Child Health Master Plan be prepared by every state. Such a plan would include first, an inventory of the number of low-income mothers and children in each county; second, a description of existing services; third, an analysis of what would be needed to fill the gaps; and fourth, a plan to coordinate in every county all children's health, education, and social-service programs.

In communities where health clinics already exist, services might be expanded. In others, new clinics would be needed. Putting all of the state plans together would lay the foundation for a *national* network of Ready-to-Learn Clinics.

Several states have already launched just such efforts. The Kentucky Education Reform Act of 1990, for example, authorized the establishment of "family service centers" in all school districts where 20 percent of the children participate in the federal school-lunch program. Hawaii's "Project Healthy Start" has one-stop centers all over the state for children and families at risk. The program also includes a home-visit plan to help parents under stress. North Carolina's "Baby Love" program gives basic health care to pregnant women through "maternity care coordinators" who act as ombudsmen, guiding the client into the system. Results of "Baby Love" are impressive. In 1988, the mortality rate for infants born to women not in the program was 14.7 percent; for those in the program it was 9.6 percent.

Over the last twenty years, the Robert Wood Johnson Foundation has led the way in creating school-based health clinics. Today, there are twenty-four projects in seventeen states. These clinics, often headed by nurse-practitioners, have been remarkably effective in diagnosing childhood diseases, immunizing children, and improving health, especially among the poor. In Hartford, Connecticut, for example, two nurse-practitioners work with a part-time pediatrician, part-time den-

27

tists, and several health aides in a trailer at the back of an elementary school. By identifying health problems early, the center has improved child health and reduced school absences. In Galveston, Texas, nurse-practitioners identify previously untreated problems and refer students to medical care facilities in the area. In Cambridge, Massachusetts, a model project offers full pediatric services in an elementary school. "A healthy child attends school more," noted pediatrician Philip Porter. "A child who attends school more learns more."

How might the Ready-to-Learn Clinics be financed? State funding will be required. But before more money is appropriated, the duplication and overlap of existing services should be eliminated. In one state, for example, we found that thirty-seven different state agencies are administering one hundred-sixty separate programs for children and youth in seven different departments.[47] Coordinating existing health programs would, we are convinced, save literally millions of dollars, redirecting resources away from paperwork and toward people.

In Seattle, a new child-health project is doing just that. The city is integrating all money currently earmarked for children's services—including community health centers, hospitals, school districts, city health departments, mental health, and substance abuse programs. The purpose is "to streamline the organization and delivery of child-health services," says Michael Beachler at the Robert Wood Johnson Foundation, which supports the program's administration and planning. Again, we believe that taking inventory and coordinating existing resources would provide funding for the one-stop clinics we propose.

Still, more money will be needed, and the federal government should help. Currently, states receive $530 million from the federally funded Community and Migrant Health Centers program that supports two thousand centers, serving six million needy clients from coast to coast. Expanding this program would make it possible for Community and Migrant Health Centers to establish satellite Ready-to-Learn Clinics in unserved areas in their regions.

Another federal project—the Maternal and Child Health Block Grant program—also gives about $500 million annually to states to help fund

28

health services on a discretionary basis. To ensure that Ready-to-Learn Clinics are located in *every* community where needed, appropriations for this program also should be increased. However, as an important prerequisite, we recommend that states receive additional funds for these two programs *only* after the need has been clearly documented, *and* after a plan to coordinate existing resources has been developed—based on the state's county-by-county inventory.

As for staffing, we suggest that every Ready-to-Learn Clinic be headed by a health professional—a nurse-practitioner, professional midwife, or senior nurse—with a private physician or public health officer available for referral. Ideally, the staff also would include a social worker, a parent educator, and trained volunteers—retirees or college students, for example—to help with parent education and transportation. Home visits would be a central feature. Further, Ready-to-Learn Clinics would train parents who, in turn, would teach other parents what they have learned.

In Houston, a program called "De Madres a Madres" (From Mothers to Mothers) illustrates just how effective trained parents can be. This project uses women volunteers who received eight hours of intensive training. In one barrio, where 40 percent of the pregnant women have belated or no prenatal care, fifty women—bank clerks, waitresses, and school cafeteria staff—work with three thousand pregnant women, visiting them in their homes, guiding them to prenatal care, accompanying them to fill out papers. Results are impressive. Among the clients tracked, not one has had a low-birthweight baby. And in their next pregnancy, most of the mothers begin prenatal care early.

Finding well-qualified health professionals to staff Ready-to-Learn Clinics will be a challenge. But here again, Washington can help. Since 1970, the National Health Service Corps has given scholarships and loans to about thirteen thousand students—doctors, nurses, and other professionals—who agree to work in underserved communities, after training.[48] Recently, due to budget cuts, participation has dramatically declined. Given the urgent need, we strongly recommend that the National Health Service Corps be expanded. We also urge that priority be given to the recruitment of nurse-practitioners and professional mid-wives, skilled health workers who can provide quality maternal and child care.

The ''one-stop health clinic'' idea is now widely recognized as the only way to go. Just two years ago, President Bush signed into law a pilot project called the Comprehensive Child Development Program, which provides for one-stop health centers. Services include basic health care for children such as screening, immunization, early detection programs, and nutrition services. For parents, there is prenatal care, parent education, and a referral service. First-year appropriations were $25 million, supporting programs in twenty-four cities. Another $20 million will be added in 1992 to support twenty-one additional sites—all stressing the integration of services for mothers and children.

Hundreds of other programs can be found from coast to coast. A comprehensive health center in Jackson, Mississippi, for example, provides primary-care services, acute sick-care, screening, and immunization to about four thousand preschoolers every year. The Jackson-Hinds Center has prenatal care and delivery, a birthing center, and nutrition counseling, as well as referrals to drug and alcohol treatment centers. A satellite health clinic located in a local high school is regarded as a model. However, the director, Dr. Aaron Shirley, reports that the clinic's budget has been frozen for the last five years ''even though we're seeing more and more patients in poverty who can pay only 20 to 40 percent of the actual costs, if that much.'' He added, ''Poverty is increasing, but our funding is staying the same. Also, medical costs are rising. Our equipment is twenty years old, but we don't have enough money to make capital improvements. We have just enough to keep the door open.''[49]

TW Cares, a community health center in Denton, Texas, is located in a low-income housing project where mostly single mothers and children live. The program was launched two years ago by Texas Woman's University College of Nursing after the closing of a public hospital left many with no place to go. The program provides primary care, educates families about health, and refers clients to other social-service providers. If children are very ill, they see a doctor. In cases of abuse or neglect, families are sent to the Department of Human Services. A dental clinic is located on site. Last year, $30,000 worth of dental services were donated. TW Cares works with the local school, where one-third of the children have no health insurance and go to the school nurse for help.

The conclusion is clear: The first and most essential step in a national ready-to-learn campaign is a healthy start. For this to be accomplished, good education, good nutrition, and access to basic health care for all mothers and babies are required. ''We absolutely cannot afford to wait until the school bell rings to attend to our children's health,'' states a report from the National Health/Education Consortium. ''We need to start thinking of immunizations, well-child care and health screenings, proper food, and prevention of health problems as being just as important to education as books and pencils and chalkboards and teachers. We need to act swiftly—and we need to act boldly. There is no time to waste.''[50]

EMPOWERED PARENTS

HOME IS THE FIRST CLASSROOM. Parents are the first and most essential teachers. All children, to become ready for school, must live in a secure environment where language promotes learning. To achieve these goals, we urge mothers and fathers to read aloud to their children, tell them stories, take them on excursions, and celebrate the language of the arts. We propose, as well, that each of the fifty states launch a parent education program, with a common guidebook. Finally, we recommend that preschool PTAs be organized to give support to parents and build a bridge between home and school.

Next to physical well-being, a child's most pressing, most persistent need is bonding, the social and emotional connection that results from loving relationships with others. Human beings have an absolute requirement for social intercourse from the first moments of life, according to biologist Mary E. Clark.[1] How else can we explain the reaching out to others, the innate urge for language, the formation of friendships, and the intensity of family ties? When children are socially and emotionally supported by caring adults, their prospects for learning are wonderfully enhanced. If, however, children are denied this supportive home environment during the first years of life, it will be more difficult for them to succeed fully in school.

Love promotes learning. Even physical contact such as holding and hugging advances the well-being of little children. In a remarkable experiment at the University of Miami Medical School, premature infants, who usually have little direct physical contact with adults, were massaged gently for fifteen minutes several times a day. These babies gained 45 percent more weight than did those who were left alone. The nervous systems of the massaged infants matured more rapidly, they were discharged from the hospital earlier, and they did better on follow-up tests of motor and mental ability. Other studies involving other primates strongly reveal the powerful need of infants for physical affection.[2]

The point is beyond dispute. After health comes human bonding. The two are bundled up together. Children who receive stable, responsive care are more likely to develop trust, empathy, curiosity, and confidence—feelings so essential to social development and to learning.[3] If affection is withheld, prospects for healthy growth decline.

A caring environment builds emotional maturity and social confidence, keys to school readiness, but such an environment is also especially consequential to language development. It's in the early years when youngsters become linguistically empowered, when they miraculously learn to express feelings and ideas. Every child, to be educationally successful, needs a language-rich environment, one in which adults speak well, listen attentively, and read aloud every day.

The miracle of language actually begins *in utero*, as the unborn infant hears sounds, monitors the mother's voice, and listens to the rhythm of her heart. In fact, the bones in the middle ear—the hammer, anvil, and stirrup—are the only bones that are fully formed at birth. Diane Ackerman paints this picture: "The womb is a snug, familiar landscape, an envelope of rhythmic warmth, and the mother's heartbeat a steady clarion of safety. Do we ever forget that sound? When babies begin talking, their first words are usually the same sounds repeated: Mama, Papa, boo-boo."[4]

Following birth, the baby's language explodes. First come cries and coos, then isolated phonemes and imitative words, culminating in simple sentences that so delight the grown-ups (figure 4). By the time a child heads off to school, at about age five, he or she has, on average, a vocabulary of more than three thousand words. A child has acquired, too, a truly awesome capacity to use words both as signs of affection and as weapons of assault. It's amazing how small children, with no formal instruction, become so linguistically empowered. Childhood is for language, as essayist Lewis Thomas puts it.[5]

Language, without question, is the key to learning. Children who fail to develop adequate speech and language skills in the first years of life

Figure 4

Language Development:
The Child's Ability to Think and Talk

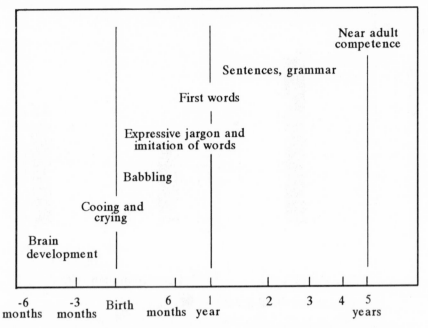

SOURCE: Adapted from *Human Development: From Conception Through Adolescence* by Kurt W. Fischer and Arlyne Lazerson (New York: W.H. Freeman and Company, 1984), 365.

are up to six times more likely to experience reading problems in school than those who receive adequate stimulation.[6] Hannah Nuba, a librarian in the New York Public Library, notes that one wonderful way parents can promote language *and* bonding is through reading, beginning right at birth. "I am often asked by expectant or new parents about the best time for introducing books to young children," she says. "My answer is always: Right now. . . . Gentle, relaxed conversation (albeit one-sided at first) provides a rich learning environment for the infant from the beginning, while tending to have a soothing effect on the . . . parent as well."[7]

That's the ideal. The reality is, however, that vast numbers of children grow up in environments that are language poor. They hear curt commands, not mind-enriching conversations. They receive careless re-

Figure 5

Three- to Five-Year-Olds Whose Parents
Regularly Engage in Literacy Activities with Them

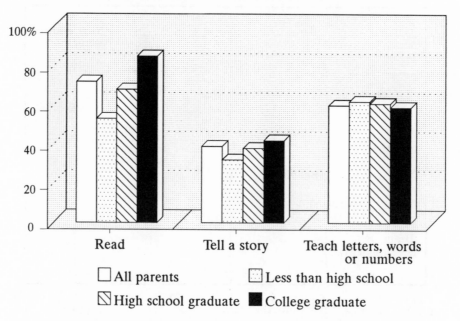

Note: Excluding those enrolled in kindergarten.

SOURCE: National Center for Education Statistics, 1991, in *The National Education Goals Report, 1991* (Washington, DC: The National Education Goals Panel, 1991), 36.

sponses to their questions, or they are ignored altogether. In fact, according to one survey, parents talk to their children, on average, just a few minutes every day, usually giving orders.[8] Further, a U.S. Department of Education report recently revealed that nearly 30 percent of today's parents do *not* regularly read aloud to their children. Nearly 60 percent don't tell their children stories (figure 5).[9]

In many homes, it's even hard to find a children's book. One teacher wrote: "It shocks me that each year I meet new parents who haven't been reading to their children simply because they don't know they should." Another wrote: "In my district, most parents are only in their teens. They simply do not know how to prepare their child for school, because they themselves are still children." One kindergarten teacher wrote: "I talk with parents about reading to their children and many say

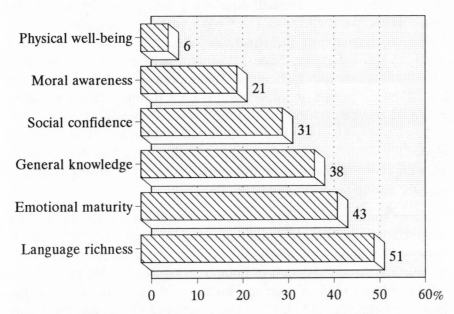

Figure 6

Teachers Reporting "Serious Problems"
in Six Dimensions of Readiness

Physical well-being	6
Moral awareness	21
Social confidence	31
General knowledge	38
Emotional maturity	43
Language richness	51

0   10   20   30   40   50   60%

SOURCE: The Carnegie Foundation for the Advancement of Teaching, National Survey of Kindergarten Teachers, 1991.

they don't have books at home or they aren't sure what stories are appropriate.''

Kindergarten teachers are especially aware of just how closely linked language is to learning, and many are deeply troubled by the poor speech patterns of their students. One teacher wrote: ''It's really frustrating to see children who simply can't communicate. They can't form simple sentences or carry on any kind of conversation at all. It's like they have been starved for words.'' Another said, ''What young children need most is a caring home, just spending time together. They also need a language-rich environment where there is lots of talk and reading. Parents need to know that a two-year-old can learn rapidly, and all parents should talk to their children—have conversations in the home.'' Even more revealing, when we asked the teachers what problem *most* restricted the school readiness, overwhelmingly they said ''deficiency in language'' (figure 6).

If every child is to be ready for school, language must become a priority in every home. Parents, as well as day-care providers, must speak frequently to children, listen for responses, answer questions, and read aloud to them at least one-half hour every day, preferably longer. To help parents, we suggest, as a part of the national campaign, that the Children's Division of the American Library Association prepare a Ready-to-Learn Reading Series, one with new and classic literature geared especially to preschoolers. The American Library Association has already prepared an attractive brochure listing children's books, called "Becoming a Lifetime Reader." It recommends selections such as Eric Carle's *The Very Hungry Caterpillar,* Margaret Wise Brown's *Goodnight Moon,* and Beatrix Potter's classic *The Tale of Peter Rabbit.* This creative effort might be expanded into a larger listing of books appropriate for preschoolers.

The new series could be placed in libraries all across the land and be distributed to parents by pediatricians or by employers. It could be made available on loan at schools, synagogues, churches, even at supermarkets. A new program in Boston called Read to Me gives a colorful children's book to each new mother in the hospital. Other distribution programs could build on the experience of this and the highly effective Reading Is Fundamental program, which distributes books to children nationwide.

Literacy in the richest, fullest sense means learning to communicate not just verbally but nonverbally as well, since little children, even before becoming fluent in the symbol system we call words, respond powerfully to music, dance, and the visual arts. They are drawn, almost instinctively it seems, to bright, interestingly shaped objects. They are soothed by music, and they respond to rhythm and dance. Long before they can speak clearly, children can draw, move rhythmically, and sing. A painting, a playful poem read aloud, a song's beat, a dance step are among the countless symbols that enrich a child's world. Without the language we call art, children simply cannot fully convey their thoughts or vividly express their feelings.

Harvard psychologist Howard Gardner, in his provocative book *Frames of Mind,* reminds us that we as human beings not only have verbal

Table 4

Parents Reporting That They Regularly
Engage in Arts Activities with Their Three- to Five-Year-Old Children
(By Parental Education)

	ALL PARENTS	LESS THAN HIGH SCHOOL EDUCATION	HIGH SCHOOL GRADUATE OR SOME COLLEGE EDUCATION	COLLEGE GRADUATE
Teach songs or music	39%	38%	39%	41%
Engage in arts and crafts	34	34	31	42

Note: Parent or another adult family member.

SOURCE: National Center for Education Statistics, 1991, in *The National Education Goals Report: Building a Nation of Learners* (Washington, DC: National Education Goals Panel, 1991), 36.

intelligence but we have, as well, interpersonal intelligence, spatial intelligence, musical intelligence, and kinesthetic intelligence.[10] This is true, of course, for little children, who should regularly be able to explore the beauty of the world around them—discovering sights and sounds, touching flowers, viewing the symmetry of bridges, observing the shapes of buildings, looking at raindrops on the window pane, watching the floating clouds, and in cities and towns visiting libraries and museums, art galleries, aquariums, and zoos.

The arts are, to put it simply, an essential language which must be developed if school readiness is to be achieved. Yet, according to a recent survey, only 39 percent of parents regularly engage in music activities with their children. Only about one-third engage in arts and crafts activities (table 4).[11]

Overwhelmingly, parents want to do right by their children. The problem is that in our fast-paced world, mothers and fathers find it difficult to spend time with their children, to talk with them at leisure, to help expand their world. In too many homes, parents are more distracted than engaged. We find it revealing, for example, that half of the nation's adults, according to a Louis Harris survey, feel that the quality of family life in this country has deteriorated. Three out of four say that

Table 5

Parents' Attitudes Toward Children and Family Life

	PERCENTAGE AGREEING
Problems affecting children are worse than when I was growing up	76%
It is a problem finding enough time to spend with children	60
Family life is worse than it was when I was growing up	52
Parents generally are doing a good job in giving their children values	47

SOURCE: Louis Harris and Associates, Inc., 1986.

problems affecting children are worse today than when they were growing up; 60 percent confirm that it is difficult to find enough time for their children (table 5).[12]

Mealtime used to be an occasion when family members came together not just for food but to talk and exchange ideas. Around the table—amidst the chatter and confusion—children heard new words, received new messages and, according to sociologist Robert N. Bellah, learned "the terms of civil discourse."[13] But even mealtime may be an endangered tradition. Today, when children are hungry, they often just help themselves to snacks. No time to talk or listen. Thanks to the microwave oven, people now eat and run. A recent survey revealed that about 30 percent of today's families do not regularly have dinner together.[14]

Several years ago, The Carnegie Foundation surveyed five thousand fifth- and eighth-graders to get a sense of family life. Responses were revealing, and disturbing. Sixty percent said they wish they could spend more time with their mothers and fathers. Nearly one-third said their families never sit down to eat a meal together. One suburban youngster told us: "We usually don't eat dinner at the regular time because we never see each other. We're always coming and going, and there's no time to sit down together to eat."

40

Time and time again kindergarten teachers referred to the poor home life they see, describing their students as "neglected," and "living disconnected lives." One teacher said: "Parents really do want to spend more time with their children, but they simply are trying to do too much, without help. It's very hard for them to fit the pieces together." Pediatrician T. Berry Brazelton reinforces the point: "There is every indication that families in the U.S. are trying to handle more than they can alone. The tensions created by the necessity of both parents working pervades their lives. The parents feel there is not enough time left for caring for their children."[15]

Surely time is a problem. But inadequate parenting skill is a problem, too. We have in this country a prevailing myth that parenting is something almost anyone can do. It's either "innate" or easily picked up from relatives and friends. Sometimes that's the way it works. There are parents who have the time, resources, and knowledge needed to provide rich, rewarding experiences for their children. Their instincts lead them, as they have led other parents in countless previous generations, to respond to their children in stimulating and supportive ways.

More often, however, parents raise their children as they have been raised, which may not be good enough. We're convinced that many parents would welcome helpful guidance, especially as it relates to school readiness. Further, kindergarten teachers, when asked what would do the most to improve the readiness of children, responded most frequently, "Parent education" (figure 7). One teacher argued: "Parents need to be educated and helped. They need to feel good about themselves—then they'll be better parents in the long run." Another teacher put the issue even more directly: "I think America's children would be ready for school if this country would have *mandatory* parent education classes for all parents of newborns."

Mandating may be going too far. However, we believe that an *optional* parent education program should be made available in every school, with each state guaranteeing access to all mothers and fathers of preschool children. The goal would be to *empower* parents, helping them

41

Figure 7

Which One of the Following Goals Would You Rank above All Others as the Most Important?

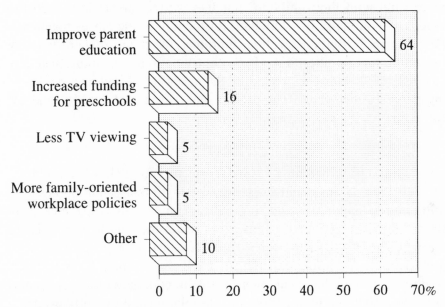

Note: Other suggestions equalled 10 percent.

SOURCE: The Carnegie Foundation for the Advancement of Teaching, National Survey of Kindergarten Teachers, 1991.

learn more about child-rearing while, at the same time, building a bridge between the home and school. Further, parenting classes should be held at places convenient to parents—in churches, synagogues, Head Start centers, community buildings, housing projects, and work sites, for example. To cover costs, state support would help. In addition, participants might pay on a fee-for-service basis, using a sliding scale based on income.

Several states have led the way. Minnesota's Early Childhood Family Education Program, one of the oldest and most comprehensive in the nation, operates in each of the state's 380 school districts, serving families with children under age five. Currently, 180,000 children, along with parents, attend a two-hour session every week—usually at a school, occasionally at a work site. During the first hour, parents and children meet together with a teacher-observer who gives child-development guidance. The second hour, parents meet alone to discuss successes and frustrations. One mother said, "It is almost like having another family, because even when I am having problems, or when I need a little time to talk, they're always there."[16]

Missouri's Parents as Teachers program serves all families with children under the age of three in all of the state's 542 districts. Participants are recruited at childbirth classes, doctors' offices, and health clinics. A video called "Born to Learn" is shown to mothers during hospital visits. Approximately sixty thousand parents are enrolled. The program monitors the health of children and provides home visits by parent educators. Funded by the state and by private foundations at an average cost of about $350 per year per family, Parents as Teachers is reported to have made a dramatic impact, increasing the knowledge of parents and the school performance of children.[17] This success has led to the establishment of a National Center for Parents as Teachers in St. Louis, and other states are developing the program.

In Arkansas, a program called HIPPY—Home Instruction Program for Preschool Youngsters—reaches forty-five hundred preschoolers and their parents. Parents use guidebooks to teach their youngsters for fifteen minutes a day, five days a week, thirty weeks a year, for two years. A parent—often a mother who has already completed the course— makes home visits and monitors the progress of other mothers and children. The state funds 60 percent of the program, with local communities contributing the rest. HIPPY is now in sixteen states, from Michigan to Texas, serving more than nineteen thousand families. HIPPY USA, a project of the National Council of Jewish Women, provides training and technical assistance to new and ongoing programs.[18]

One parent involved in HIPPY said: "I never thought I could teach my child anything. I never knew I had anything to teach her. HIPPY showed me I do. It made me my child's first teacher." Another parent noted: "I always knew I could feed and clothe my son, but I never tried to teach him anything because anything I taught him would be wrong." A

Table 6

Models of State Parent Education Programs

STATE	ELIGIBILITY	NUMBER SERVED	BUDGET
Arkansas HIPPY	Educationally at-risk 4–5 year olds	11,000 in Arkansas, 8,000 more nationwide	$9 million
Maryland Family Support Centers	Teenage parents with children 0–3 years old	2,500 parents and children	$7.5 million
Minnesota Early Childhood Family Education	All parents with children 0–5 years old	185,000 parents and children	$25.2 million
Missouri Parents as Teachers (PAT)	All parents with children 0–3 years old	60,000 families	$11.4 million
Oregon Together for Children	At-risk families with children 0–8 years old	6,000 families, with 376 families receiving intensive services	$266,000+

SOURCE: Compiled by The Carnegie Foundation for the Advancement of Teaching.

third said: "It has taught my son his shapes and colors, how to pay attention to someone when they are reading to him, and how to follow directions. It has taught us to have a better relationship. It allowed us to spend time together that normally we would not have." A Little Rock mother gave this testimonial: "The HIPPY program has given my son the educational advantages he needed to prepare him to enter into the school system. Some parents have no idea how to teach their children. And in this case, that parent was me. But HIPPY has made another life worth living" (table 6).[19]

A parent education program in *every* state would contribute greatly to the ready-to-learn campaign. Further, a *national* effort would make it possible for states to work together, learning from each other and developing a high-quality curriculum. After all, good parenting is the same in Oregon and Ohio. Rather than ask fifty states to go down separate paths, why not have a collaborative parent education approach, one that reflects best practice? Further, since 20 percent of American families move each year, a more uniform approach to parent education would make it possible for those who relocate to find a similar program wherever they live.

Therefore, we suggest that a national "Parent Guide" be prepared by a consortium of education groups, led by the National Association for the Education of Young Children and the Council of Chief State School Officers. The goal: to ensure quality and continuity from school to school and state to state. The guide should be written in clear, concise, jargon-free language, and be understandable to all parents, especially those who have limited reading skills. We also urge that parenting programs include a literacy component to help parents who have not yet learned to read.

The National Center for Family Literacy, for example, helps parents and children learn to read together. In a Kentucky project, where the center started, mothers and children come to school three days a week on the same bus. They eat meals together in the cafeteria, and while the children are in one classroom, parents learn to read in another. Parents also serve as school volunteers while their children play. Then they travel home and read together. Sharon Darling, president of the center, said: "We are trying to get parents to raise their literacy skills so that they can, in fact, support education in the home."[20] One mother wrote: "For years I wanted to go back to school but I always had plenty of excuses and reasons not to. I was afraid if I pursued my dream my children might somehow be left behind. And then you placed a bridge that supported all of us, allowing us to dream together, learn together, and achieve together."[21]

Finally, all communities should organize a preschool PTA—encouraged by the National Congress of Parents and Teachers—to give support to parents and build a bridge between home and school. Today many mothers and fathers feel isolated. They have little or no communication with the school until it's time to register their child. Even then the encounter is often fleeting and unrewarding. To promote school readiness, all parents of preschoolers should be able to talk with other parents and have contact with teachers, too. Without such interaction, parents, children, and schools are placed at a disadvantage. When we asked one kindergarten teacher whether her children are ready for school, she replied: "I'm personally more concerned about whether schools are ready for the children."

The National Congress of Parents and Teachers has gained great credibility in this country. The organization has displayed a deep commitment to education, to families, and most especially to a strong partnership between home and school. The PTA traces its roots back to 1897, when a new organization called the National Conference of Mothers was established to educate mothers of young children about child development. By expanding its efforts to include preschool parents, the National PTA would, in a very real sense, be returning to its roots. Already, the PTA has 192 preschool affiliates nationwide.

Lakewood, Ohio, has an informal network for preschool parents, with five hundred participating families. The program is organized by blocks within school districts so parents can get to know neighbors. There are eight such neighborhood subsections. Each conducts social, educational, and support activities for parents. Parents continue to sign up, and the group keeps growing. "The networking is important," said president Becky Sammon. "It is important to know that you are not alone whether you are a working mom or a single mom and that when you have a problem you have someone to call and talk to. You borrow ideas from other parents. Some may seem silly, like 'how should your child respond to a bully at preschool?' But these are topics important to preschool parents."

Historian Will Durant has called the family the nucleus of civilization.[22] It remains the key to education, too. And every child needs the care and guidance good parenting can provide. For all children to come to school ready to learn, we must empower parents.

The Third Step

QUALITY PRESCHOOL

LAST FALL more than four million children started school, not as kindergartners or first-graders, but as three- and four-year-olds off to their first day of "preschool." They are among the eight million youngsters under the age of five who enroll each year in some form of child care outside the home.[1] The quality of this experience will consequentially shape a child's readiness for school, especially the disadvantaged. The Business Roundtable states the case precisely: "While it is not a silver bullet, the evidence is very strong that a quality, developmentally appropriate preschool program for disadvantaged children can significantly reduce . . . poor school performance."[2]

Quality preschool can be helpful to *all* children. We recommend, therefore, that Head Start become an entitlement program and urge, as well, that every school district offer a preschool program for all other three- and four-year-olds on a fee-for-service basis. We also recommend that day-care services for infants and toddlers be expanded, and that licensing standards for child-care programs be established and adopted by all states. Finally, we propose that community colleges take the lead in promoting quality child care by offering a new, associate, preschool professional degree and by forming a collaborative relationship with child-care programs in their regions.

Placing a young child in the care of others is a difficult decision most often born of necessity. A mother of a three-year-old told us: "I hate dropping my son off at 7:30 every morning. We hardly have time to grab a bite of breakfast, and when we meet again at night there's only time for fast-food and then it's off to bed. But I'm a single parent and frankly have no choice." Another working mother said: "It's just a fact of life that my husband and I are going to work. We need two incomes

Table 7

Preschoolers in Various Child-Care Settings

	1977	1991
With a parent	25%	28%
With a relative	31	19
Family day care	23	20
Child-care center	13	28
Caregiver in own home	7	3

SOURCE: Barbara Willer et al., *The Demand and Supply of Child Care in 1990* (Washington, DC: National Association for the Education of Young Children, 1991), 44; National Child Care Survey 1990 and Profile of Child-Care Settings.

to have anything approaching a comfortable life. That means our little girl has to go to day care.'' Another single mother noted: ''The debate over the pros and cons of day care has become tiresome. I *need* the help. That's the reality of the situation.''[3]

Child care in America has grown dramatically. Since the 1970s, the number of children placed in care outside the home has increased four-fold. The location and type of care have shifted, too, and today 28 percent of all employed mothers place their children in child-care centers.[4] That's up 15 percent since 1977. Nineteen percent now depend on relatives for such care, compared with 31 percent in 1977. The percentage of those using a caregiver in the home has dropped from 7 to 3 percent, while the number of families providing their own care has increased slightly (table 7).

The ideal is for children, especially the very young, to be cared for by their parents. The value of the parent-child relationship cannot be overstated. Child care by others outside the home, however, has become a necessity for many parents and the good news is that *quality* child care can, in fact, be beneficial. Youngsters in such programs make new friends, develop language skills, learn to share, and create imaginary worlds. They gain social confidence and develop a sense of right and wrong, increasing prospects for school success. Psychologist Jean Piaget maintained that a well-developed child needs both adult *and* peer relationships—the former to learn respect for the social order and conventions, the latter to develop feelings of "moral reciprocity," kindness, cooperation, and justice.[5]

Tiffany Field, at the University of Miami Medical School, found that children who spent time in high-quality child care were better adjusted emotionally and socially in elementary school than were those without such experience. They had more friends, and the more active they were in the program, the more highly they were rated on emotional well-being, popularity, attractiveness, and assertiveness.[6] In a Syracuse, New York, study, children from low-income families who participated in a comprehensive child-care and family-support program were compared with those who did not. Program participants, especially the girls, did better in school. Boys not participating committed almost four times more disciplinary offenses than participating boys.[7]

Kindergarten teachers, we discovered, firmly support high-quality child care. When asked what would "most improve" the school readiness of children, the second most popular suggestion teachers made was "preschool education." Equally impressive was the frequency with which teachers wrote about the value of preschool. One teacher noted: "The most important step this country can take is to make sure each child is offered the opportunity for preschool." Another added: "From my own experience, it's clear that children who have had preschool come to kindergarten with better language skills, better motor capabilities, and a broad base of knowledge."

Formal child care here in the United States can be traced back to the early nineteenth century when charity workers in the growing cities sought to protect and educate children of the working poor.[8] By mid-century, the idea of the "day nursery," inspired by the French *crèche*, became the preferred choice. The Helen Day Nursery in Chicago, for example, saw itself as "a place where children who need shelter and protection by day or night may be cared for during the mother's working hours; a place which shall provide temporary refuge in emergency; and an industrial, educational, and social center for mothers from which shall emanate standards of respectable living."[9] Experimental kindergartens and, later, nursery schools for children of middle-class parents rounded out the early-childhood education scene.

It was not until the Great Depression that group care was attempted on a large scale. Under the Federal Recovery Act and Works Project Administration, nearly two thousand "free nursery schools" for two- to four-year-olds were organized through public school districts. Designed at first to create jobs for the unemployed, these nurseries were rapidly superseded by a new system of full-fledged day-care centers, built quickly during the Second World War so mothers could be mobilized as wartime workers. Most of these closed when hostilities ceased.

During the 1960s—a decade when almost one-quarter of the nation's mothers with preschool children entered the labor force—early-childhood education exploded. Sparked by policy debates and pilot programs, kindergartens expanded in almost all the states, accommodating two-thirds of the nation's five-year-olds. Tuition-supported nursery schools proliferated, with the enrollment of three- and four-year-olds rising from 800,000 in 1965 to 1,150,000 in 1970. Head Start, a centerpiece of the Johnson Administration's War on Poverty, offered preschool to poor children.

Twenty years ago, the White House Conference on Children declared that child care was one of the most pressing problems facing American families.[10] Since then, little progress has been made. What we have today is a truly chaotic "nonsystem," one parents enter with little confidence, little knowledge, and even less power to change. Low-income families are at a special disadvantage. Consider that in families with incomes of $30,000 or less, only about 40 percent of the children are in preschool. For affluent families, it's 75 percent (figure 8). Further, for poor families the cost of preschool consumes, on average, 23 percent of the monthly income. For high-income families the number is 10 percent.[11]

Most parents who have children in child care are ambivalent, at best. Many who say they are satisfied with arrangements they now have are still looking for improvements. That's not surprising. Nearly one in four families have piecemeal arrangements and are forced to use two

50

Figure 8

Three- to Five-Year-Olds
Enrolled in Preschool, by Family Income

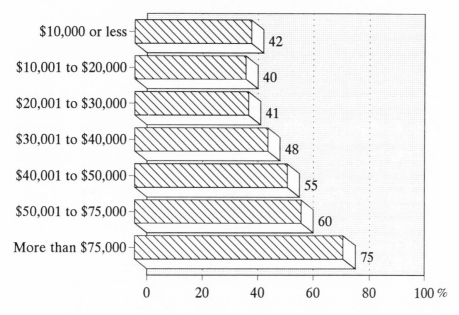

SOURCE: National Center for Education Statistics, 1991, in *The National Education Goals Report:
          Building a Nation of Learners* (Washington, DC: National Education Goals Panel, 1991), 37.

different providers in a single day, according to a Carnegie Foundation
survey of parents. One mother told us that the only preschool program
she could find was across the city in exactly the opposite direction from
her work. "To make matters worse," she added, "preschool ends at 2
o'clock and I don't get off until 5:30 p.m."

For a very long time this country has been of two minds on the subject
of child care. With the number of women in the workplace growing,
the need is apparent. On the other hand, commitment to "traditional
family values" has created a climate of caution, even some resistance.
As a result, today the United States stands almost alone among industrialized nations in its failure to have a national child-care policy. Indeed, this country has a smaller proportion of its four-year-old children
in preschool programs than many other countries, despite the high pro-

portion of mothers working outside the home.[12] Columbia University researcher Sheila Kamerman states: "The U.S. lags far behind almost all the major advanced industrialized countries with regard to the supply, quality, and affordability of out-of-home child-care services."[13]

By contrast, European countries give high priority to preschool.[14] Ninety-seven percent of the three- to five-year-olds in France, for example, are in such programs. In Belgium, the figure is 95 percent; and in Germany it's 80 percent.[15] Children in these countries typically are cared for in government-regulated and subsidized programs, at little or no cost. Many centers are open from 6 a.m. to 8 p.m. to accommodate working parents.

In Reggio Emilia, Italy, for example, child-care programs are available beginning in infancy. The first school, for children up to age three, is called the *asilo nido*, meaning "safe nest," and the second school, for children up to age six, is called the *scuola materna*, meaning "maternal school." There are regular meetings of parents and teachers, and child care is seen as an accepted part of community life, an alliance dedicated to children. These preschools look like greenhouses filled with plants, art, and bright open spaces; program directors believe that the physical environment is perhaps as important as the teacher.[16]

In Copenhagen, preschool children go on daily neighborhood excursions. Inga Kraus, an early childhood expert, gives this description: "Children are very much part of the street scene. Groups of ten or twenty can be seen every day on public transportation facilities—buses, trains. No one grumbles when a group climbs aboard, despite the fact that they leave very little room. It is just an everyday thing. Groups of young children walking through the city are a common sight. Young ones hold on to a rope and the very youngest are in wagons. This caravan travels everywhere—negotiating traffic and public facilities."[17] Care for children is a public concern.

If America is really serious about school readiness, quality child care must become a priority, and the place to begin is Head Start. Since 1965, this federally supported program has provided preschool education primarily to disadvantaged three- and four-year-olds. Today, about two thousand Head Start centers serve 548,000 children. The goal is to build self-esteem, provide good nutrition, and give to every youngster the learning experiences needed to succeed in school. Each center designs its own program and involves parents, bringing families together. "The whole point of Head Start," says Cornell University's Urie Bronfenbrenner, "is to build a sense of community."[18]

In Ulster County, New York, Head Start begins at 9 a.m, with children greeting each other, engaging in a half-hour of free play at various "learning stations." Then comes breakfast, a time for language as well as food—with teachers discussing topics introduced by children. After brushing teeth, children spend an hour on a special theme, guided by a teacher. They then play outdoors, walking through the neighborhood, climbing an obstacle course, or visiting the local library for a story. At mealtime, children pass the food, pour their own beverages from pint-sized pitchers, learn about utensils. After lunch comes rest time. Next, children listen to stories and music, and then work independently or together on puzzles and other projects. Foster grandparents often come to visit.

The Sunnyvale Head Start in Santa Clara County, California, shares space with Young World, a private day-care provider, as well as with a day-care program in the local school. Another Santa Clara program is housed in a homeless shelter. San Jose's Head Start serves refugees from Cambodia and from Latin America, helping disadvantaged children while also teaching English and work skills to older members of the family.[19]

On the Flathead Indian Reservation in northwestern Montana, 120 Salish Kootenai youngsters are enrolled in six Head Start programs, four hours every day. Children learn basic hygiene. They participate in a family-style breakfast with older people, a time for conversation. The children sing, listen to stories, and go to different learning stations for sand and water play, drama, science, or other learning themes. Parents help plan cultural activities. Many fathers participate, as do grandparents, called "elders." Jeanne Christopher, the director, says elders sit quietly in the classroom while children move in and out, engaging them in activities, sharing work. Each center has its own tipi. In the spring there is a reservation-wide pow-wow, an ''intergenerational sharing time,'' as Christopher calls it. ''Elders drum for the children. Children go to the homes of elders for stories.'' Tribal values are preserved, connections are forged.

Head Start works. Head Start children in Philadelphia were, according to a nine-year study, less frequently retained, had better attendance rates in school, and were less likely to have serious school problems. A California study found that Head Start participants scored higher on tests for verbal achievement, perceptual reasoning, and social competence.[20] The Orangeburg, South Carolina, school district established an all-day preschool for disadvantaged four-year-olds. Test scores in the district increased as much as 200 percent in language arts, math, and reading. School officials are convinced that early intervention made the difference.[21] Indeed, a summary of hundreds of Head Start studies concluded that children enrolled in the program make significant gains in test scores and have better health.[22]

The widely reported research on Head Start by David Weikart at the High/Scope Foundation's Perry Preschool Project in Ypsilanti, Michigan, concluded that every dollar invested in quality preschool education saves $4.75 in reduced welfare benefits, reduced criminal costs, and increased earnings and tax revenues.[23] Clearly, Head Start is an investment that pays off, educationally *and* financially (figure 9).[24] The Committee for Economic Development states the case for early intervention: ''Business people know that it is less expensive to prevent failure than to try to correct it later. Early intervention for poor children from conception to age five has been shown to be a highly cost-effective strategy for reducing later expenditures on a wide variety of health, developmental, and educational problems that often interfere with learning.''[25]

Not surprisingly, teachers, too, confirm the value of preschool. One kindergarten teacher wrote: ''Children entering my class who have had preschool, especially Head Start, are better adjusted.'' Another noted, ''Preschool programs like Head Start fill a void and provide rich experiences—nutrition, socialization, and speech development. Such pro-

54

Figure 9

Benefits of Early Education

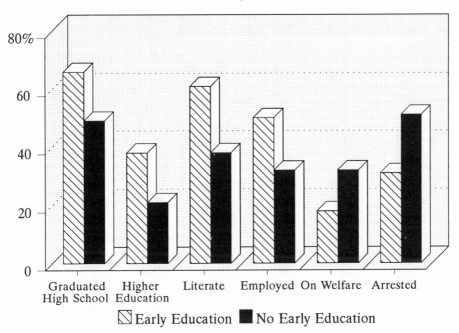

Note: By age 19.

SOURCE: *The School Readiness Act of 1991, S.9-1-1*, May 1991.

grams surely should be expanded so all children who need them could be helped.''

In spite of all the evidence of its value, a quarter-century after Head Start was authorized by Congress, *two-thirds* of the eligible children are still not served (table 8).[26] This is inexcusable. How can we justify denying access to a program that brings such benefit to children? It is, in a sense, like withholding a vaccine that would protect them from a dreaded disease.

If America is really serious about school readiness—if the first education goal is to be something more than an empty slogan—Head Start must be fully funded, surely by 1995. The program should be designated an ''entitlement'' to ensure, at last, that *all* eligible children will

Table 8

Children Participating in Head Start

AGE	CHILDREN ENROLLED	INCOME-ELIGIBLE CHILDREN
TOTAL	**577,741**	**2,044,200**
3	161,000	915,000
4	375,000	852,000
5	41,741	277,200

SOURCE: Anne Stewart, "Head Start: Percentage of Eligible Children Served and Recent Expansions," *CRS Report for Congress* (Washington, DC: Congressional Research Service, the Library of Congress, 30 July 1991), CRS–4.

be served. According to our best estimates, this would increase Head Start's appropriation from $2 billion to $8.3 billion,[27] an investment that would pay off handsomely in the long run.

Beyond full funding, Head Start also should be closely tied to elementary schools to ensure continuity for the children and common purposes for teachers. When Head Start began, its leaders quite understandably insisted on independence. They worried that schools would exercise too much control—dictating curriculum, forcing preschoolers into rigid classroom procedures, making the program "too academic." During the intervening years, however, Head Start has established its autonomy and demonstrated its value beyond doubt. Further, most school educators have become convinced of the value of preschool. The time has come, therefore, for the programs to be more closely joined.

Locating Head Start at or near a public school is one way to achieve closer ties. Already, about 20 percent of all programs are located in school facilities. Further, teachers at both levels should work together to design a common curriculum, one that focuses on such qualities as physical well-being, emotional maturity, language richness, and general knowledge, as well as social confidence and moral awareness. We also urge that Head Start and elementary school teachers meet occasionally to compare notes. The value of such exchanges would flow in both directions and would especially benefit children.

In Alexandria, Virginia, George Washington Head Start meets in a junior high school. Teachers work together. Older students read to preschoolers from 3:00 p.m. to 5:30 p.m. In Dunkirk, New York, Head Start is housed in a public elementary school, making it possible for preschool and kindergarten teachers to meet at the end of each year to discuss the children. In Cleveland, Ohio, schools host an open house for Head Start families. "We initiated a dialogue with the school system to help children make a smooth transition from Head Start to kindergarten," said Jethro Cason, the Head Start director.

Disadvantaged children, unquestionably, can be helped by preschool. But surely other youngsters can benefit, too. Several years ago, Yale child-care authority Edward Zigler, founder of Head Start, proposed the establishment of a year-round preschool program in *every* public elementary school. The child-care system must become "part of the very structure of our society," Zigler said, "tied to a known, widely used societal institution."[28] This is an idea whose time has come.

Classes for four-year-olds in the nation's public schools have quadrupled in the past decade. Today, 15 percent of all school districts offer such programs.[29] Further, in a Carnegie Foundation survey of parents, more than half of all respondents said they favored publicly funded preschools for four-year-olds whose parents choose to enroll them.[30] We conclude, therefore, that every school district should establish a preschool program for children not covered by Head Start, with the program being financed partly by the state and partly on a fee-for-service basis using a sliding scale.

In Independence, Missouri, two elementary schools—models of what Zigler calls "The School of the Twenty-First Century"—have all-day child care for children aged three to five. At the Sycamore Hills School, preschoolers are in a program located in the school itself. Parents of newborns in the neighborhood receive advice and are helped to find day care for toddlers. High school students enroll in child-development classes at the center and volunteer as child-care assistants. Parents are charged a fee according to their ability to pay.[31]

Hartford, Connecticut, schools operate a similar program with state support. At Betances School, for example, one mother with two youngsters takes both her six-year-old son and three-year-old daughter to school together. The children play for half an hour. Then at 8:00 a.m., the six-year-old goes to his first-grade class and the three-year-old enters preschool. At three in the afternoon, they meet again to play, work on puzzles, and read in a school-supervised program. The children are picked up at 6:00 p.m. "It's comforting to know that my children are in a safe place all day and just down the street from where we live," the mother said.[32]

The Bellevue, Washington, school district has a range of tuition-based preschool and child-care programs; eight hundred children participate. One center is located on the high-school campus, others in elementary schools. Classes with twenty children are staffed by two teachers. Preschool programs are closely coordinated with the elementary school, and by the year 2000, Bellevue plans to have a preschool in each elementary school.

Preschool for three- and four-year-olds should become universally available, but the most frustrating problem many parents face is finding quality care for younger children—infants and toddlers. "Infant care" is, in fact, the greatest child-care challenge facing the nation today, according to the National Academy of Sciences.[33] Yet, the first years of life are the most crucial to learning. It will be impossible to meet the nation's first education goal if our youngest and most vulnerable children do not have a stimulating environment, with loving care. Home care surely is preferred, but many parents simply must place their children in the care of others, which often brings frustration.

One mother we talked with said that before returning to work, she wanted to place her new baby in a home-care environment, but no relatives were available to help. She thought about hiring a nanny, but could not afford it. Then her choice was between a private day-care home or a center. Unfortunately, the family home she liked best had a long waiting list. "I had my name on lists for nine months," she re-

58

called, "and it was within ten days of when I had to go back to work, and I had no place to keep the baby. I finally found one place that could take her for several months, but it's all so temporary."

Federal legislation may offer some relief. The new Child Care and Development Block Grant program, approved by Congress and signed into law by President Bush in 1990, gives money to families to support day care. Parents receive certificates and vouchers to help pay for the child-care service of their choice, either in the home or away. Part of the money in the new legislation—nearly 20 percent—has been set aside for states to expand day-care services and support *new* initiatives.

Minnesota has earmarked the funds for training, accrediting, and licensing child-care providers, and to create new programs, including those for children with special needs. Arizona plans to support toddler care, and Florida will train child-care providers. New Mexico is focusing on family-support services. Ohio, on the other hand, is setting up a full-time infant care program in high schools. Tennessee is expanding its family "home networks" by recruiting senior citizens to care for infants and toddlers in their homes. New Jersey has launched Good-Starts, a comprehensive early-childhood initiative targeted to serve young children who are eligible for, but not served by, Head Start. Montana will use its grant to expand existing day-care facilities and start new ones.[34]

Other nongovernmental initiatives are also underway. One of the most impressive is the National Family Day Care Project sponsored by the National Council of Jewish Women. Thirty demonstration sites in twenty states use community volunteers to recruit and train new child-care providers. In Baltimore, for example, a program called "Side by Side" helps day-care centers become licensed, well equipped, and well staffed. The result: hundreds of additional children have been placed in licensed day-care homes. Worcester, Massachusetts, produced a videotape to inform new day-care providers about local resources and regulations. Birmingham, Alabama, started a training program on public television for local early-childhood professionals. In Miami, a roving van called a Resourcemobile, with educational toys and a full-time early-childhood specialist, offers assistance to child-care providers.

While expanding day-care services, states must be equally concerned about standards. After all, we're talking about our youngest, most vulnerable children. It is unacceptable that today almost 40 percent of those now in out-of-home care are *not* protected by any state regulations,[35] with many programs even operating "underground" to avoid regulation. Today, states regulate almost everything, from drivers to realtors, but when it comes to protecting children, uniform standards have not been officially endorsed. Surely states should be able to say something more to the parents than "buyer beware."

Regarding child-care standards, each state has gone off in its own direction, resulting in a patchwork of requirements. Consider child-to-staff ratios. For one-year-olds, the maximum permitted in California is 4 to 1; in Delaware it is 7 to 1. For four-year-olds, the maximum ratio in Illinois is 10 to 1; in Delaware, it is 15 to 1. Space requirements vary, too. One state specifies thirty-five square feet per child; in another it's only three. One state has well-defined training requirements for day-care workers; another has none.[36]

Even *within* a state, program standards can be unequal. We visited one day-care center in New Jersey with a well-deserved reputation for quality. It was open from 8 a.m. to 6 p.m. Four classes were offered—one each for two-, three-, four-, and five-year-olds. Class size ranged from fifteen to twenty-two children, and the child-to-adult ratio was five-to-one for the two-year-olds, slightly higher for older youngsters. Rooms were large and cheerful. Children had easy access to toys and books. The playground outside was attractive and well equipped. Children came from a broad range of family backgrounds. Teachers were well trained and reasonably well paid. Turnover was minimal.

At another center, just ten miles down the road, the atmosphere was chaotic. Doors were locked to prevent children from straying. One staff person "supervised" ten three-year-olds in a room with few toys and a hard-surfaced floor. With a rapid turnover of hassled, demoralized,

60

poorly paid, and poorly trained teachers, children were rarely taught and seldom comforted. The directors were defensive. Outsiders were not encouraged to visit. Could parents have known what was happening here? Why should any child have to spend time at such a place? How long will this country continue to give such a low priority to children?

We recommend that a National Forum on Child-Care Standards be convened by the National Association for the Education of Young Children to define a more uniform licensing system for day-care centers and preschools, with quality the key. Fortunately, a foundation exists on which such standards can be built. The National Association for the Education of Young Children has developed a set of high standards and has a well-defined process for accrediting, on a voluntary basis, early childhood programs with ten or more children. The National Association for Family Day Care has a parallel set of regulations for family day-care homes. Seven other national groups have established standards, including the American Academy of Pediatrics and the Public Health Association, which have jointly published a report on standards for child-care facilities that cover a wide range of topics—from security to playground equipment.

In developing national child-care standards, "day care" and "preschool" should be viewed as complementary programs, with general standards that apply to both. Historically, early childhood specialists have organized themselves into competing camps—with the "day-care" people on one side, the "preschoolers" on the other, as if little children can be forced into bureaucratic boxes. We strongly urge that the long-standing barriers between "care" and "education" be broken down. We need common standards that apply to day care *and* preschool, ones that view the needs of the *whole* child—from physical well-being to moral awareness. Years ago, professor Bettye Caldwell at the University of Arkansas coined a wonderfully descriptive term— "educare"—that captures precisely what we have in mind. Let's put the focus on children.

In the end, high-quality child care depends on high-quality staff. Even the best-formulated standards will be useless without skilled teachers. The time has come for America to acknowledge that the first years of

61

learning matter most and that we simply must give more dignity and more status to those who shape the lives of little children.

The first step is better pay. Caring for young children is an awesome responsibility. It is unconscionable that the average hourly salary for early childhood educators is less than $6.00 an hour, not much more than the minimum wage teenagers receive for serving up french fries. The average annual salary is now about $11,000—a 25-percent decline in real wages since the mid-1970s.[37] Is it any wonder that the annual turnover among preschool staff has tripled in the last decade, to well over 40 percent in many places?[38]

Several states have attempted to correct the situation. Michigan, for example, links salaries for preschool teachers to those of elementary teachers. Connecticut and Minnesota provide state funds to help compensate preschool staff. But these are exceptions. Nationwide, we continue to pay our lowest wages to our most essential teachers. Former Secretary of Commerce Peter G. Peterson challenged our priorities when he asked: ''Why do we continue to devote so many resources to comforting us at the end of life . . . while we pay a Head Start teacher less than $10,000 to prepare us at the beginning of life?''[39]

Beyond better pay, preschool teachers also must be better trained. In France, early childhood teachers have the equivalent of a master's degree.[40] Directors of child-care centers are pediatric nurses with training in public health *and* child development. Staff assistants usually have two years of college, plus a two-year course in child development. In contrast, here in the United States only about one-third of the preschool teachers have had any child-related training, and just 24 percent have the Child Development Associate credential, as recommended by the National Association for the Education of Young Children. Even worse, thirty-one states require *no* training for home-care providers.[41] Clearly, it is time for day-care providers and preschool teachers to be professionally prepared.

Community colleges are uniquely positioned to take the lead in promoting preschool education—both in training professionals and in building partnerships with programs in their region. Specifically, we urge that a special degree program be offered by every community college, called Child Care Professional. Further, we propose that every one of the more than twelve hundred community colleges offer continuing education for all child-care workers in their service areas.[42] Community colleges might also recruit mid-career professionals and retirees into preschool education and give "preschool education" scholarships to gifted high school students, thus strengthening their mission of "building communities."

Dutchess Community College in New York grants an associate degree in early childhood education. About half of those who graduate teach at child-care centers; the rest transfer to four-year programs. Cuyahoga Community College in Cleveland also has such a degree, providing placement and referral for graduates in child-care centers in the area. Miami-Dade Community College has a sixty-two credit child-care degree program, with a base in the liberal arts, a core of early childhood courses, electives, and practical field experience. The college has established a "satellite" public school on its north campus to help preschoolers make the transition to elementary school. Standing Rock Community College in Fort Yates, North Dakota, plans to offer a two-year degree program in early childhood education beginning in 1992. This college, located on an Indian reservation, will include courses in liberal arts and in child development as advocated by the National Association for the Education of Young Children, and will give students practical experience in a child-care setting.

To complete the network, community colleges might establish a relationship with selected four-year colleges and universities engaged in pioneering laboratory and research work in early education. The Center for Infants and Parents at Teachers College, Columbia University, for example, offers a special program on parent-focused infant care—blending training, practice, and research—for master's and doctoral students. All students work closely with parents during their on-site practicum. The Elliot-Pearson Department of Child Study at Tufts University has undergraduate and graduate early-childhood degree programs that focus on applied child development, offering an independent program with ten courses in early childhood education and a liberal arts core, coupled with an intensive practice. A preschool on the Tufts campus for youngsters ages two to six serves as a laboratory.

The Bank Street College of Graduate Education in New York offers graduate programs in early-childhood education, with an infancy program and a day-care program. The Child Family Center, which serves children six months to four years of age, is a demonstration site for teacher training in infant care. The director, Margo Hammond, observed: "These small family groupings provide ample opportunities for language development and social and emotional growth. There is always an adult to answer questions, and respond to children." What's being proposed in this chapter is a new professional network for preschools, one in which all child-care programs are affiliated informally with a community college which could, in turn, work closely with a senior institution that has a strong commitment to preschool children.

We are at a point in this nation where most children will spend thousands of hours in day-care and preschool programs before they enter school, an experience that will profoundly shape the quality of their education—and their lives. If all children are to be ready to learn, we must begin to give status to our most important teachers. A Colorado kindergarten teacher put it succinctly: "If every child could have a high-quality preschool year, many of our problems would be solved . . . and I'd be thrilled."

The Fourth Step

A RESPONSIVE WORKPLACE

JOB PRESSURES, last-minute shopping, chauffeuring back and forth, paying bills, and a myriad of other chores keep parents on the go and often out of touch with their children. Here's how one single mother described the complications of her life: "I feel the biggest problem in the home is what I call 'after-work burnout.' I know this is an important time for my child. I should go over his school day and homework before it gets late and he becomes tired. I tell myself this every day, but by the end of my workday, all I can think about is getting home and relaxing before starting the evening chores."[1]

If every child is to come to school ready to learn, we must have family-friendly work policies. We recommend in this chapter a four-part strategy for employers to consider: first, we call for a parental leave program, so parents can create strong emotional bonds with their newborns. Second, we propose flextime and job-sharing arrangements, so that home and family obligations can be better blended. Third, we suggest that employers help with child care. Finally, we recommend "parent days," so that mothers and fathers may visit children at child-care centers.

In yesterday's agrarian society, families lived on farms, in villages, or in small towns. "Work life" and "home life" were intertwined. Mothers, fathers, and children worked side by side, forming a common economic enterprise and producing, with the help of friends and neighbors, food and other staples needed to survive.[2] Life was hard, hours long, and financial rewards meager. Still, the social and economic dimensions of family life were connected, with children often serving as apprentices to parents or other mentors, understanding what parents actually did at work.

Figure 10

Mothers in the Paid Labor Force, 1970–1990

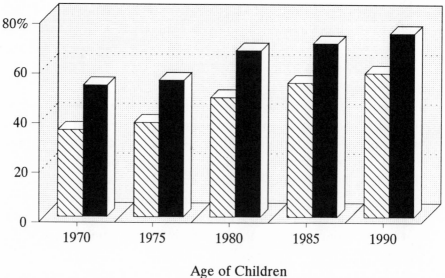

Age of Children

◨ Less than 6 ■ 6-17

SOURCE: U.S. Department of Labor, Bureau of Labor Statistics, *Handbook of Labor Statistics*, Bulletin 2340, 1989, 244; and unpublished data from March 1990 Current Population Survey.

All this has changed. "The family economy has disappeared almost completely," according to the Carnegie Council on Children.[3] Today, fewer than 3 percent of American families live on farms. Most parents work outside the home. Consider these facts: In 1975, about seven million children under the age of six had mothers in the work force. Today, the number has almost doubled. Nearly 60 percent of all mothers with preschool children and approximately half of those with children under age one are now working (figure 10).

The gap between work and family life has widened, isolating children from the adult world, putting them in second place. Sociologist Arlie Hochschild describes the situation this way: "For all the talk about the importance of children, the cultural climate has become subtly less hospitable to parents who put children first. This is not because parents love children less, but because a 'job culture' has expanded at the expense of a 'family culture.' "[4] A kindergarten teacher in rural Missouri made a similar observation: "I believe parents love their children, but in today's society everyone works and they are just plain tired. After all, the job comes first."

In a *Better Homes and Gardens* survey, 77 percent of the respondents said they felt that family life was in trouble. Seventy-six percent said they would be willing to reduce their income or slow their career development in order to spend more time with their children.[5]

According to another recent report, American parents overwhelmingly feel they do not spend enough time with their children.[6] One parent wrote: "Next to divorce, the greatest problem I see with today's parents is that we are becoming 'stressed out'! That is, trying to juggle meaningful careers, children, community and church activities, household chores, and school. I do not feel we are shirking our responsibilities as parents, but we're simply taking on too much. I seriously believe this will affect our families in years to come."[7]

The point is clear: It is simply impossible to separate work and family life. If children are to get support at home and be prepared for school, family-friendly policies in the workplace are needed—policies that not only strengthen the role of parents but also give care and guidance to young children. A kindergarten teacher observed: "Since so many families are affected by dual careers, I firmly believe employers must be more concerned about family needs. If children are to be ready for school, we need more on-site day care, more parental leave, more job sharing. After all, workers are parents, too."

How should we proceed? How can the obligations of parenting and the workplace be reconciled to the benefit of both? As a first essential step, we strongly recommend that mothers and fathers be given time off to be with their babies following the child's birth. Making it possible for parents to interact with their newborn is basic—essential to the well-being of the child. Psychologist Burton White has repeatedly emphasized the importance of *parents* being with their children, especially in the first weeks of life.[8] This is a time for establishing strong emotional bonds.

Fifty years ago, the U.S. Department of Labor recommended that all working mothers be given six weeks of prenatal leave and eight weeks of leave after the baby comes—without sacrificing job and seniority benefits.[9] Parental leave legislation has been introduced and debated in Congress each year since 1985—and is widely supported by the public. Nearly 80 percent of Americans believe that employers should be required to give new parents at least unpaid leave.[10] Yet a half century after this visionary concept was officially proposed, little progress has been made. Former U.S. Secretary of Labor William Brock says: "It's just incredible that we have seen the feminization of the work force with no more adaptation than we have had."[11]

The United States is, in fact, the *only* industrialized country that does not have a national policy guaranteeing maternity and infant-care leave. Today, more than 80 countries in Asia, North and South America, Africa, Europe, and the Middle East have some form of government-mandated parental or maternity leave.[12] Most of our major trade partners guarantee job protection. They provide pay for leave as well. In many countries, working mothers are able to take an average of four to five months of *paid* leave, receiving anywhere from 60 to 100 percent of their salaries.

In Finland, working women get thirty-five weeks of parental leave with full salary. In Japan, women have the right to a three-month leave at 60 percent of their pay (table 9). In Germany, mothers who have worked for at least nine months are eligible for a fully paid leave beginning six weeks before a baby's birth and ending eight weeks after it. Ninety percent of German women take another four-month leave at a more modest rate of pay. Mothers who work in the public sector can actually take several years of unpaid leave while maintaining job protection.[13] Some countries also give paid leave to fathers.

Those opposing parental leave in the United States worry about a governmentally imposed mandate. They wonder where it will lead. Fur-

Table 9

International Comparisons of Parental Leave Policies

COUNTRY	WEEKS OF PARENTAL LEAVE	NUMBER OF PAID WEEKS	PERCENT OF NORMAL PAY
Austria	16–52	20	100%
Canada	17–41	15	60
Finland	35	35	100
France	18	16	90
Germany	14–26	11–19	100
Italy	22–48	22	80
Japan	12	12	60
Sweden	12–51	38	90

SOURCE: Women at Work, International Labor Office Global Survey, *CDF Reports* (May 1991): 2.

ther, it is feared that such a policy will cause special difficulties for small businesses. Also, there is concern about the costs. A recent survey, however, suggests that, in the long run, a parental leave policy can actually *save* money through increased employee retention.[14] Sociologist Robert N. Bellah and his colleagues, in *The Good Society,* declare: "It might appear at the moment, when economic competitiveness is such an obsession, that Americans 'can't afford' to think about the family if it will in any way hinder our economic efficiency. Nothing could be more shortsighted. In the long run our economic life . . . depends on the quality of people."[15]

Again, parental leave is crucial. It's a policy that would strengthen the child's emotional and social well-being and promote learning. We specifically recommend, therefore, that employers should offer parents of newborn or newly adopted children at least twelve weeks of unpaid leave. It is simply unacceptable that here in America where half the work force is female, new mothers are so penalized. It is deeply troubling that they are forced to return to work before fully recovering from childbirth, required to leave their babies in the care of others before emotional bonds are well established, or even deprived of their liveli-

69

hoods. Consider also how this undermines the fulfillment of the nation's ready-to-learn objective.

Some companies are demonstrating what can and should be done. IBM allows working parents to take up to three years of parental leave. Merck & Co. has an eighteen-month leave policy. Even small businesses such as Joy Cone, a company in Hermitage, Pennsylvania, that produces most of the nation's ice cream cones, gives employees up to a year and a half of unpaid parental leave, with job protection.[16] John Hancock Mutual Life Insurance Co., Hechinger, Ohio Bell, Arthur Andersen, US Sprint, AT&T, and Johnson & Johnson all offer employees one year of unpaid leave. Other companies—Lotus Development Corporation, for example—give employees a shorter period of *paid* parental and childbirth disability leave.[17]

The SAS Institute, a software company in Cary, North Carolina, provides up to a year of unpaid leave for child care or other personal reasons.[18] Human resources director David Russo says that the company endorses the policy's use by either parent. "A lot of businesses look for all the reasons not to get involved with child care. Jim Goodnight [SAS founder] looked at why we *should* get involved," he said.[19] Jane Helwig, a co-founder of SAS, herself a working parent, said that the difficulties she faced in balancing her roles as mother and executive paved the way for these family-friendly policies. Helwig describes the company's philosophy this way: "The feeling has always been that if you treat employees as though they make a difference to the company, they *will* make a difference."[20]

US West, the communications company in Englewood, Colorado, has one of the country's most generous parental leave policies: up to two years of unpaid leave for time with newborns and young children.[21] Board chairman Jack MacAllister calls this policy "an investment." "Our children are our future," he says. "Our choices are to invest our energy in educating them or to become a nation without skilled workers, unable to compete in the global economy, a people whose progress is hampered by social inequity."[22]

Hemmings Motor News, a magazine published in Bennington, Vermont, has a variety of family-friendly policies, including six weeks of paid parental leave, plus another six months of unpaid leave for mothers *and* fathers. When Charles Waters and his wife had their first child, they took advantage of the policy which allowed Mr. Waters to spend two or three days each week in the office and the remaining days at home with the baby. "It gave me an opportunity to spend some precious time with my children when they were infants, to bond with the babies," says Waters. "And by spending a few days a week in the office, I was still able to keep up with my work. The company's family policies and flexibility really helped our family."

In the absence of federal legislation, states are creating their own policies. In Oregon, a parental leave program requires companies with twenty-five or more employees to give parents twelve weeks of annual leave, including time off to care for sick family members. Oregon also mandates maternity leave. Health-insurance benefits are maintained during leave periods, and employees have the right to return to a former job or to a comparable position after leave.[23]

Rhode Island's parental leave legislation, which applies to all employers with fifty or more workers, is regarded as a model. Under this program, employees who work at least thirty hours a week are eligible for thirteen weeks of parental leave, with their health-insurance benefits maintained. Employees who take such leave are required to pay premiums for health-care coverage into escrow accounts, but are subsequently reimbursed upon returning to their previous position—a right that is guaranteed.[24]

Beyond offering parental leave, employers can also help strengthen family life by allowing parents to modify the typical 9-to-5 routine with "flextime" arrangements. One mother in Washington State said: "Our school district began offering a preschool program for four-year-olds. I wanted my daughter to enroll, but the program ends at 3:00 p.m. and I work until 5:00 p.m."[25] In such circumstances, parents are forced to spend lots of time on the phone, checking with neighbors or caregivers, interrupting their work. Older children who fill in as baby-sitters often call parents at work, seeking help. Frustration builds, productivity declines. When schedules are adjusted, parents can spend more time with children, and less time on personal business at work.

In 1974, the federal government became the nation's first major employer to offer a more flexible work schedule to employees. Seven years later, one-third of a million federal workers were participating in one of the 1,554 alternative work-schedule programs in twenty different agencies. In a survey of employees' opinions, nine out of ten said flexibility was important in helping them solve family and work problems, in caring for sick children, in reducing baby-sitting expenses, and in allowing them to spend more time with their children.[26] Today, 19 percent of the federal work force uses flexible schedules. Managers believe such reforms are essential to attract and retain a quality work force.[27]

In the private sector, Pitney Bowes in Stamford, Connecticut, allows individual departments to work out their own schedules. All employees are required to be at work during a core period from 10:00 a.m. to 2:00 p.m.[28] Before and after this period flexible arrangements are permitted. IBM also has flextime. One design-engineer father in Kingston, New York, arranged his work schedule so that he could meet his daughter at the school bus. Proctor & Gamble in Cincinnati, Ohio, allows hourly employees to alter work schedules by one hour at either end of the day. "These arrangements were provided to meet the changing needs of employees," Terry Loftus, a company spokesman, said. "The work setting is different than twenty years ago. There are more working moms, and we have broadened the company's perceptions to meet these changing needs."[29] In 1988, nearly 12 percent of all workers in the country were on some sort of flexible arrangement.[30]

"Job sharing"—another flexible approach—allows two part-time employees to staff one full-time position. At American Express, for example, one middle-level manager took the company's eight-week leave when she gave birth to her first child, then returned to work full-time, placing her daughter in day care for fifty hours a week. After several months, she began to feel that life for her and her baby was out of balance. The company agreed that she and a colleague, also a mid-level

72

manager, could split one job. Thus, both employees were able to spend part of each week with the family and part at work.[31] Part-time work and "telecommuting"—doing work from home—also help families, and such arrangements will increase.

Employers also should consider offering "parent days" to their workers, occasions when employees are given time off to be with their children to share experiences and bring their separate worlds together. After all, workers are excused to vote or serve on juries, sometimes for weeks. Why not give working mothers and fathers at least two days each year to be with their children, especially the first day of day care or preschool, to get to know the teachers and become acquainted with the other kids, and simply get close to their own children? It is really rather sad the way so many youngsters go off to preschools or day-care centers early in the morning while parents go off to work, with little time together. And first-hand encounters are the only way parents can really know what is going on in their children's lives.

In Massachusetts, Governor William F. Weld recently announced that parents who are state employees may spend time in their children's schools "to visit classroom teachers, to volunteer in schools, and to serve in school governance." He also asked other employers to provide released time for such activities, beginning at the start of each school year. "I have challenged business to redefine the model of what constitutes good corporate citizenship," he added.[32] Proctor & Gamble gives parents half-day vacations to attend afternoon programs at their children's schools or to participate in school events.[33] North Carolina National Bank gives employees two hours of paid leave each week to work in schools, participate in their children's school activities, or confer with teachers. The bank also matches, dollar for dollar, an employee's financial contribution to his or her child's school.[34] "Successful parenting is as challenging as successful banking," says an official.

Two years ago, *Hemmings Motor News* began "education participation days" by giving employees two days off each year to visit schools, participate in volunteer activities, or observe classes. The program did

73

not evolve from employee pressures; rather, it was initiated by the publication's owners and managers, who are committed to family-friendly policies. The number of employees participating during the first year was small, but the company continued the program and urged employees to participate, out of concern for Vermont's children, families, and schools.[35]

Another approach is to bring children right to the workplace, offering a child-care service close to where parents work. This idea is not new. As early as 1816, industrialist Robert Owen created the first employer-based child-care center in Scotland, establishing an "Infant School" at his mill for children ages one to twelve. During our Civil War, businesses that produced ammunition and soldiers' clothing created on-site nurseries to care for the children of women employees. Day-care centers were established at hospitals and war-related businesses during the First World War. During the Second World War, over two thousand day-care centers were created at worksites, using government funds provided through the Lanham Act;[36] however, these were considered "emergency measures" and were dropped when America returned to a peacetime economy.

As recently as twenty years ago, child care at the worksite was limited to about two hundred companies. Today, about five thousand businesses offer some form of child-care arrangement—dramatic evidence of the growing corporate concern for the quality of family life.[37] Significantly, two-thirds of Americans believe employers should, in fact, take the lead in helping families meet child-care needs. Seventy-one percent feel that the private sector should become involved in child care and 45 percent say that business should fund such programs, even if that would mean reductions in wages and benefits.[38]

Ten years ago, the city of Irvine, California, promised its citizens that by 1992 adequate child care would be available to all parents. By conducting a door-to-door survey, the city found numerous gaps in such services. In response, Irvine's child-care spaces have increased more than 80 percent over the past five years. This includes a $1.2 million

74

Table 10

Employers Reporting Benefits of On-Site Day Care

RESULT	PERCENTAGE
Better morale	90%
Easier recruitment	85
Improved public relations	85
Less turnover	65
Less absenteeism	53
Greater productivity	49

SOURCE: National Commission for Employment Policy, "Employer Strategies for a Changing Labor Force: A Primer on Innovative Programs and Policies," Research Report, 1982, 77.

municipally funded child-care facility in Irvine's new Civic Center, which reserves space for the children of city employees. Irvine provides after-school care for latchkey children and offers incentives to developers to include child-care space in all new commercial and business projects.[39]

Parents who have access to on-site child care are more productive, take less leave time, and have better attitudes toward work.[40] A comprehensive survey of 415 companies revealed that on-site child care brought beneficial results: morale improved and absenteeism declined (table 10).[41] In another survey, Nyloncraft, Inc., of Mishawaka, Indiana, reported that they had major reductions in turnover rates and a drop in absenteeism to less than 3 percent as a result of its child-care programs. Lincoln National Corporation in Fort Wayne, Indiana, said its child-care program led to reduced absenteeism and improved productivity. At Mercy Richards Hospital, 34 percent of employees said that the child-care center was a factor in their accepting jobs at the hospital.[42]

Patagonia, an outdoor clothing and equipment manufacturer in Ventura, California, has an on-site child-care center for eighty infants and children. Yvon Chouinard, Patagonia's founder and co-owner, said the company supports the center because of worker satisfaction and low turnover. "Frankly, to replace an employee costs thousands of dollars, so if we can save just a few employees over the year, we're making money," he said. "And that doesn't even factor in lost time due to distractions from child-care problems, improved morale, and lots of other things. Plus, we get suppliers who come into the cafeteria and see mothers eating lunch with their kids. And it has a great effect on them. They trust a company that does that. In fact, most of them want to come to work here. It's good advertising, that's for sure. And it's just plain good business.''[43] Consider again how critically important such time together is to parents and especially to children. For a child, having lunch with a parent—uninterrupted time to talk and to share the excitement and troubles of the day—can be emotionally reassuring.

The law firm of Akin, Gump, Hauer, and Feld also has its own child-care center, "the place for kids," across the street from its downtown Washington office, with an emergency child-care service that operates seven days a week. Susan Suarez, director of the program, has outings to parks, picnics at the zoo, swimming during the summer, and movies—all involving expeditions by public transportation, with babies in strollers and the young children holding hands. Attorney Harriet Lipkin's two young children, Joshua and Stephanie, see the center as "their place." If Lipkin's regular child-care arrangements fall through, if her sitter is sick or on vacation, the children can go to the center. The firm also has a child-care committee, a parents' newsletter called "Small Talk," plus a parental support group that has monthly brown-bag lunches, with speakers.[44]

Ben and Jerry's, the ice-cream company in Waterbury, Vermont, has their Children's Center, located nearby in a renovated farmhouse, that cares for children from six weeks to six years of age. "We have all found that having children at the workplace is a very humanizing experience,'' said Beth Wallace, the director. "Our toddlers and preschoolers visit the plant and see everything from ice-cream production to shipping and processing. When infants are in the yard and the other children are playing, parents and other workers wave at them from the windows. There are lots of smiling faces on both sides.''[45]

Some companies, particularly small ones with fewer than 250 employees, may find it difficult to provide on-site care. They may be sympathetic to parents' needs, but find it economically unfeasible to set up

76

their own in-house child-care facilities. Perhaps the best approach for such businesses is a collaborative arrangement, one in which several companies jointly sponsor a child-care center. Alternatively, these companies can give their employees child-care grants to subsidize the costs of care at a local center, or at the very least provide a referral service to advise parents about child-care options.

IBM has set up a $22 million fund to increase the supply and improve the quality of child-care programs. The aim of this initiative is to increase the range of options for employees and make IBM "a good neighbor."[46] To receive support, new child-care centers must meet accreditation standards set by the National Association for the Education of Young Children. A group called Care Connectors, Inc., has a computerized national "on-line child-care database" for corporate clients wanting to help employees locate day-care centers.[47]

Clearly, much is happening. Still, just 17 percent of the large firms (those with at least ten thousand employees) and only 3 percent of small businesses (those with one hundred or fewer employees) offer child-care services.[48] To forge a strong alliance between business and the ready-to-learn campaign, we recommend that a national clearinghouse be established to help employers develop family-friendly policies, gather data on the full range of programs being offered, and give special recognition to companies with creative programs. Such a clearinghouse might be established within an existing organization, such as the National Alliance of Business. We believe all companies should help their employees locate, evaluate, and if possible pay for quality child-care and preschool services either on site or at local centers.

During the past decade, America's business leaders have been vigorously involved in school reform, continually reminding us just how directly education is linked to economics and how our ability to compete in world markets is closely tied to the quality of our schools. In the coming decade, corporate America should continue to focus on school reform, of course. But special attention also must be given to families, and most especially to the care of children. As Stephen E. Ewing, president and CEO of Michigan Consolidated Gas Company, states: ''We need to change attitudes about day care so that it is no longer seen as a personal need, but rather a public expectation—a way to invest in the youth of this nation starting at birth. . . .''[49] For all children to be well prepared for school, a responsive workplace is absolutely crucial.

The Fifth Step

TELEVISION AS TEACHER

IN THE SUMMER of 1938, essayist E. B. White sat in a darkened room and watched transfixed as a big electronic box began projecting eerie, shimmering images into the world. It was White's introduction to television and in response he wrote: "I believe television is going to be the test of the modern world, and that in this new opportunity to see beyond the range of our vision, we shall discover either a new and unbearable disturbance of the general peace or a saving radiance in the sky. We shall stand or fall by television—of that I am quite sure."[1]

Next to parents, television is, perhaps, a child's most influential teacher. We therefore recommend that parents guide the viewing habits of their children. We urge as well that commercial networks air at least one hour of children's programming every week, with school-readiness messages interspersed. Third, we propose that a Ready-to-Learn cable channel be created and, finally, that a national conference be convened to explore how, during the decade of the nineties, television can contribute to the educational enrichment of preschool children.

The amount of time children spend watching television is awesome. A six-month-old infant, peering through the rails of a crib, views television, on average, about one and a half hours every day. A five-year-old watches an hour a day more. By the time the child sets foot in a kindergarten classroom, he or she is likely to have spent more than *four thousand hours* in front of this electronic teacher. All told, the nation's nineteen million preschoolers watch about fourteen *billion* hours of television every year.[2]

Television sparks curiosity and opens up distant worlds to children. Through its magic, youngsters can travel to the moon or the bottom of the sea. They can visit medieval castles, take river trips, or explore imaginary lands. As researcher Genevieve Clapp wrote: "Television has opened to children worlds that have been inaccessible to previous generations. Science, history, literature, music, art, and life in other countries are available at the press of a button."[3]

Television began with such promise. In the November 1950 issue of *Good Housekeeping* one enthusiastic mother wrote: "By and large I think television is Mama's best friend . . . [and] Kukla, Fran, and Ollie are one cogent reason. . . . [Television] widens horizons. Surprisingly often it brings into the home good plays, competently acted." Further, this mother noted, an inspired TV teacher, Dr. Roy K. Marshall, talks about "earthquakes, the solar system, and nuclear fusion. . . . Seeing what he can accomplish in fifteen minutes proves the great potentialities of television in the field of education."[4]

No one can deny television's great potential, but over the past thirty years, commercial television's great promise has faded from the screen. This multibillion dollar industry has decreed that the airwaves are overwhelmingly for adults, not children. What today's children *actually* encounter every weekday afternoon is not Kukla, Fran, and Ollie or a latter-day "Dr. Marshall," but enough soap operas to flood a laundromat. Edward Palmer, author of *Television and America's Children,* has said ". . . [I]t is economically irresponsible that we fail to use television fully and well to help meet nationwide . . . educational deficiencies in all key school subjects."[5]

On Saturday morning, during the so-called "children's hour," youngsters are served a steady diet of junk-food commercials[6] and cartoons that contain, on average, twenty-six acts of violence *every sixty minutes*.[7] Newton N. Minow, former chairman of the Federal Communications Commission, recently described television as "the most important educational institution in America. . . . All of television is education," he said. "The question is, what are we teaching and what are we learning?"[8]

According to kindergarten teachers, children are learning precisely the wrong things, and the blur of images shortens attention span and reduces learning to "impressions." One teacher remarked: "I feel I have

80

to tap dance to keep their interest. Just lecturing is a sure groaner. Students just want to be passive viewers. It's frustrating to have to be ABC, CBS, and NBC when I really want to be PBS and NPR!'' Another observed, ''TV watching must be curbed. Kids no longer know how to play basic kid games.'' A third wrote: ''Television has taught children about 'Ninja Turtles,' but they have no idea what *real* turtles are. TV is a shocking case of child neglect.''

Psychologist Daniel Anderson, after exhaustively examining the research about television's impact on the mental development of children, concludes: ''Although there are questions about the degree, there's no question that television promotes violent behavior. Kids do absorb messages from television shows, but that doesn't make them good judges of the messages they're absorbing. Right now, they're showing kids a lot of violent behavior and that's reflected in kids' attitudes and outlooks.''[9] A teacher told us: ''I really believe that TV-watching stimulates aggressive behavior and decreases the ability of children to play together without some form of fighting.''

Inga Sonesson, a sociologist at Sweden's University of Lund, monitored the behavior and television-viewing tastes of two hundred children over a ten-year period. ''We found,'' she wrote, ''a clear and unmistakable statistical correlation between excessive television and video viewing on the one hand and the development of antisocial behavior and emotional problems on the other.'' Sonesson reported that six-year-olds who watched less than two hours of television daily were far less likely than those who watched more to develop learning difficulties or emotional problems. As to those who logged more television time, she noted: ''Teachers reported that these were the children who were more aggressive, more anxious, and had greater problems maintaining concentration.''[10]

Television's impact on children depends, in large measure, on whether parents control the dial. Most programs simply are not meant for little children, yet in many homes, the television is on all day long. According to a Harvard University study, 70 percent of today's parents feel

Table 11

Parental Involvement in Children's Television Viewing

Parents who guide their children's selection of programs	15%
Parents who frequently discuss programs with their children	38
Parents who often use TV as children's entertainment	66

SOURCE: Howard Taras et al., "Children's Television-Viewing Habits and the Family Environment," *American Journal of Diseases of Children,* vol. 144, no. 3 (March 1990): 359.

that children are watching too much television. Although 40 percent of parents believe that such viewing has a negative effect on their kids, pediatricians at the University of California found that barely 15 percent of parents with children between the ages of three and eight actually *guide* their children in selecting programs (table 11). Two-thirds do not frequently discuss program content with their children, and 66 percent often use television to "entertain."[11]

Occasionally, parents do set rules; some have even banned television altogether. A national campaign called "TV Busters," launched by a teacher in Plymouth, Minnesota, asks students to stop watching television for twenty days—except for news and educational programs—and to keep a record of what they do instead. The results are fascinating. When the television is turned off children spend more time "riding bicycles," "playing soccer," or "raking leaves with their fathers." Others read. To date, 37,000 children in 154 schools in 39 states have become "TV Busters." This project has been endorsed by Minnesota Governor Arne Carlson, who last year proclaimed one week in October "TV Buster Week." Why not try this in every state?

With selective viewing, television can contribute richly to school readiness. But for this to happen parents must be well informed and must guide the viewing habits of their children just as they control decisions about eating and sleeping. Peggy Charren, founder of Action for Children's Television, has been an articulate, effective voice for parent involvement. "PBS has made preschool programming a focus of their efforts," she said, "but outreach programs for audience development have not been funded. Parents and caregivers have to know about the new programs and turn them on for their children. Parents need to know about the videos that are made just for kids."[12] Charren suggests that libraries and Head Start programs provide information about children's programming.

Clearly, more and better guidance is required. We recommend, therefore, that a Ready-to-Learn television guide be published, at least monthly, listing programs on both commercial and cable channels of value to preschoolers. Recently, Public Broadcasting Service and forty-three cable companies joined to publish a monthly television guide for junior and senior high school students. The magazine, *Cable in the Classroom,* which lists programs by topic, is available to schools without charge. Let's expand this idea and create a guide for preschoolers.

ABC publishes the "ABC Learning Alliance," which is designed to "make television a true partner in learning."[13] Targeted to teachers, librarians, parents, and students, the planner describes new television programs of special interest to young people and their families. Suggested grade levels and content areas are listed, along with ideas for using television in the classroom. ABC also offers a viewer's guide for its successful "After-School Specials," a series that deals with contemporary issues. The guide includes questions for group discussion plus a list of relevant books on the topic recommended by the American Library Association. Likewise, other commercial stations as well as PBS have prepared viewer guides to special programs. These publications, designed for teachers and parents of older students, suggest the kind of guide that is needed for preschoolers.

Parental guidance is imperative, but better children's programming is needed, too. The television industry simply must acknowledge the powerful impact television has on children and accept its responsibility to its youngest audience. Tricia McLeod Robin, president of the

National Council for Families and Television, says "parents are desperate for help and television should not just be a partner in the ready-for-school campaign; it should be the leader."

Will this be the decade when television's early promise as a "saving radiance" for children is finally fulfilled?

The Federal Communications Act of 1934 sought to ensure that the airwaves would serve the best interests of all people, including children, but since then, only a few truly creative steps have been taken on the commercial networks.[14] For years, "Ding Dong School" and "Captain Kangaroo" greeted millions of little children, who heard good conversation, learned exciting lessons about life, and were enthralled that someone was talking directly to them. Sadly, these "ready-to-learn" programs fell victim to a "bottom line" mentality. Profits were placed ahead of children. It is inexcusable that, today, no commercial network airs a single regularly scheduled *educational* program for children.

PBS, on the other hand, has been more attentive to young viewers. For over a quarter of a century, "Sesame Street" has led the way. Joan Ganz Cooney, who started this remarkable program in 1968, said that the aim of "Sesame Street" was "to promote the intellectual and cultural growth of preschoolers."[15] Featuring Jim Henson's Kermit the Frog, Big Bird, the Cookie Monster, and a host of creative personalities both real and imagined, "Sesame Street" is today viewed by millions of children in more than eighty countries. This historic, pioneering effort has contributed dramatically to school readiness, and, as a splendid program, enhances learning, especially of the basic skills.

"Mister Rogers' Neighborhood" also illustrates television's "promise fulfilled." Children who spend time with Mister Rogers develop feelings of self-worth, better understand their world, learn essential skills, and stretch their imaginations. They're more likely to help another child.[16] A recent study at day-care centers in Ohio found that "Mister Rogers' Neighborhood" helps children become more cooperative, self-confident, and creative. Viewers, they found, are less aggressive than nonviewers and make greater gains in verbal skills. Teachers also noted that children become better conversationalists after viewing Mister Rogers.[17]

84

More good news: The Corporation for Public Broadcasting recently announced funding for a new thirty-minute preschool series, "The Puzzle Factory," which will teach socialization and life skills. Slated to air by 1993, "The Puzzle Factory" will feature multicultural puppets at work in a make-believe puzzle workshop, whose stories will encourage children to make choices, take risks, and experiment.[18] Celebrity guest stars, animal mascots, and a variety of other characters will appear. According to executive producer Cecily Truett: "This is a people show, and these are 'human being' lessons. The essence of this program is that people are individuals. Each of us is unique."[19]

"Reading Rainbow," another PBS program, introduces young television viewers to a book, presenting the story in rich detail. Several years ago, "Ramona," a series based on the stories of award-winning children's author Beverly Cleary, won rave reviews and a huge following. "Shining Time Station," another award-winner, featured former Beatle Ringo Starr as a train conductor. Action for Children's Television describes the show as "basic life lessons gently taught in an enchanted setting." "Long Ago and Far Away," a series featuring children's literature from foreign countries, included shows based on *The Pied Piper of Hamelin*, *The Wind in the Willows*, and Russian folktales. The response was tremendous: teachers deluged WGBH in Boston with requests for its teacher's guide.

"Barney and Friends," a new program for preschoolers scheduled for the spring of 1992, features a big purple dinosaur who has adventures with his young friends in a day-care playground and classroom. Two Dallas mothers on extended maternity leave created "Barney" when they found it impossible to find good programs for their own kids. Shari Lewis's "The Lamb Chop Play-Along" is also scheduled to premiere soon. The show is designed to encourage young children to sing, count, rhyme, and hop along with Shari and Lamb Chop.

PBS surely has been a pacesetter in children's programming. Still, commercial networks, which profoundly influence the lives of so many children, also have a role to play in helping America achieve its education goal. We recommend, therefore, that each of the major commercial broadcast networks—CBS, NBC, ABC, and Fox—offer, at an appropriate time, at least one hour of educational programming every week. Is it too much to ask each network to devote just sixty minutes of quality television every week to children?

The Children's Television Act, landmark legislation passed by Congress in 1990, signals hope. As a condition of license renewal, the new law directs stations to provide programming specifically designed to serve children, limits the amount of advertising time, establishes procedures for public accountability, and relies heavily on citizens to monitor local stations to assure compliance. Action for Children's Television has prepared a video—"It's the Law!"—to encourage just such community involvement. PBS commentator Bill Moyers declared: "If the Children's Television Act does not make a difference, we will have lost perhaps the last opportunity to save children from mindless mass communications. . . ."

A National Endowment for Children's Educational Television also has been created. We urge that Congress increase appropriations to the endowment to $20 million to fund high-quality programs, especially for preschoolers. Further, manufacturers of children's products—such as toys, cereals, and fast foods—should devote at least some of their profits to educational television. Recently, the Ronald McDonald Family Theater presented "The Wish That Changed Christmas," based on Rumer Godden's *The Story of Holly and Ivy*. Host Ronald McDonald made live appearances during breaks to reinforce story ideas and to encourage families to discover books at their local libraries. Linda Kravitz, assistant vice-president for marketing at McDonald's, says: "With literacy in America becoming an increasingly important issue, we believe that encouraging kids to read more is an appropriate role for McDonald's." This illustrates precisely what we propose.

The new act also limits commercials in children's programs to ten and a half minutes each hour on weekends, and on weekdays to twelve minutes. Cutting commercial time may reduce the bad, but fail to advance the good. While older children show less interest in commercials, three-

86

and four-year-olds often show an *increase* in attention.[20] And what do they see? According to one observer, "A child watching television today sees ads for sugared cereals, candy, snack foods, and sugared drinks in an unceasing barrage and learns nothing of the essentials for a balanced diet."[21] Peggy Charren explains the dilemma best: ". . . It seems abundantly clear that almost everyone in the TV business is still trying to figure out how to benefit *from* children instead of how to benefit children."[22]

While focusing on the length of commercials, let's also consider *content*. Specifically, every sixty-minute segment of children's programming on commercial networks should include at least one ready-to-learn message addressing the physical, social, or educational needs of children. Why not have colorful segments on nutrition, exercise, and exciting books? Why not illustrate highlights from history, interesting scientific facts, or lessons on social confidence and getting along with others? Why not feature a kindergarten teacher describing a child's first day at school?

Commercial networks have occasionally made such a commitment. From 1973 to 1985, for example, ABC aired "School House Rock," innovative mini-programs presented during the Saturday morning cartoon line-up. Through music, rhyme, and animation, children learned about grammar, math, the human body, and American history in five-minute segments called "America Rock," "Multiplication Rock," "Grammar Rock," and "Science Rock." Millions of viewers, now young adults, still remember the "Conjunction-Junction" song, and the history lessons taught by an animated Thomas Jefferson.[23]

Today, NBC airs "The More You Know," public service messages aimed at parents and children. In ten- and thirty-second spots, celebrities promote learning, parental involvement, teacher appreciation, and discourage substance abuse.[24] Children's Action Network and the American Academy of Pediatrics recently prepared "commercials" aimed at parents. They feature Robin Williams and Whoopi Goldberg, who urge parents to have their children immunized. Possibilities for ready-to-learn messages like these are almost limitless.

Cable television, a powerful, fast-growing part of the industry, also offers great possibilities for the education of young children. We have cable channels devoted exclusively to sports and weather, sex, rock music, health, and around-the-clock news. Why not have *one* cable channel devoted solely to preschool children—at least one place on the TV dial parents could turn to with confidence, one reliable source of enriching programming all day long? Further, with a Ready-to-Learn cable channel, day-care directors and preschool teachers could incorporate TV programming into their daily schedules.

Cable channels do occasionally focus on young children. The Disney Channel, for example, features "Under the Umbrella Tree," which teaches preschoolers to use the telephone and doorbell, share with their friends, and help others. "You and Me, Kid" deals with parent-child relationships, and such classics as "Winnie the Pooh," "Babar," and "Pinocchio" make up Disney's preschool line-up. Nickelodeon offers a two-hour block of preschool programs each day, from 10:00 a.m. to noon. "Eureeka's Castle" includes puppets, comedy, music, and adventure. "Sharon, Lois & Bram's Elephant Show" takes its little viewers on adventure trips accompanied by an elephant. "Fred Penner's Place" uses stories, songs, and games to entertain and educate. On the Discovery Channel, children travel to distant places and learn about animals and their habitats. The Learning Channel program "Castles" uses animation and live action. The colorful photography and clear narration capture young viewers.

The LIFETIME channel recently began airing "Your Baby and Child with Penelope Leach," which explores developmental changes in children from birth to preschool. Last fall, the Family Channel presented a one-hour special called "Discovering the First Year of Life," and features "American Baby" and "Healthy Kids" on alternate weekday afternoons. LIFETIME also features pediatrician T. Berry Brazelton in "What Every Baby Knows" and "American Family Album," programs that focus on such issues as discipline, fears, working moms, preparing for a baby, and the child's transition to preschool. "Families need value systems they can believe in," says Brazelton. "This series will give us a chance to identify value systems in different groups around the country so that parents will have some choices."

Locally produced shows also can be enriching. WCVB in Boston has created "Captain Bob," a grandfatherly man who teaches children to draw and appreciate the environment. "Jabberwocky" uses actors and puppets to entertain and educate three- to six-year-olds each week. "A Likely Story," the newest of WCVB's productions, follows a librarian and her bookmobile on adventures through "The Magic Book," encouraging four- to eight-year-olds to read. WRLK in Columbia, South Carolina, another exceptional station, produced "The Playhouse," a six-part series that emphasizes self-esteem, and "Let's Play Like," a series devoted to imagination. The pilot program recently won a "Parents' Choice" award.

Most encouraging, perhaps, is the way technology itself is changing, offering new power to parents and new learning possibilities to children. Satellites, fiber optics, and laser disks will also be tomorrow's teachers, and videocassettes are already providing learning possibilities for preschoolers. With videocassettes, parents can stop the show for discussion and repeat segments. Excellent titles for children exist, and new ones are regularly being added. *Bowker's Complete Video Directory 1990* devoted an entire volume to educational videos, many for preschoolers. Further, most libraries have video collections and the American Library Association publishes a brochure entitled, "Choosing the Best in Children's Video." We suggest that every library create a special ready-to-learn video section, so parents can easily identify appropriate titles.

With a dash of optimism, we can see the nineties as a decade when television's promise to our children finally is fulfilled. What is needed now, we believe, is a more coherent policy established not just by government but by concerned citizens and committed leaders in the industry itself. Specifically, we recommend that a National Ready-to-Learn Television Conference be convened. The proposed forum should identify issues vital to children's programming and develop strategies to improve its quality. The promise is to enrich the lives of *all* children, to give them an exciting new window to the world, with words and sounds and pictures that dramatically enhance their school readiness. Newton Minow recently said: ''A new generation now has the chance to put the vision back into television, to travel from the wasteland to the promised land, and to make television a saving radiance in the sky.''[25] We could not agree more.

The Sixth Step

NEIGHBORHOODS FOR LEARNING

BEFORE HEADING OFF TO SCHOOL, children spend lots of time outside the home, running up and down the sidewalk, climbing trees, sitting on fire hydrants, romping in the grass, scrambling in and out of discarded boxes—observing what goes on. A child's world should be a safe and friendly place, with open spaces that invite play and spark the imagination. If every child is to be well prepared for school, we must have neighborhoods for learning.

To give children the space they need for growth and exploration, we recommend that a network of well-designed outdoor and indoor parks be created in every community. We suggest, as well, that libraries, museums, and zoos establish a School Readiness Program for preschoolers. We also urge that shopping malls include in their facilities a Ready-to-Learn Center where young children can engage in play and learning. Finally, we propose a Youth Service Corps to make it possible for school and college students to serve as volunteers in children's Ready-to-Learn programs in every community.

Children give life to neighborhoods. Neighborhoods, at their best, give something back. British social critic Colin Ward noted that a community "that is really concerned with the needs of its young will make the whole environment accessible to them."[1] Yet, in our rush to build cities, towns, and suburbs, we have somehow forgotten children. We constructed glitzy banks, and hotels that look like Taj Mahals. We erected high-rise apartments and office towers that soar into the sky. We built shopping malls and we widened highways. But often there is no place left for safe, creative play.

Lewis Mumford, in *The Myth of the Machine*, reminds us that as human societies grew from small villages into large, impersonal cities, they

91

Table 12

Children Reporting That They Are "Sometimes
Scared" When Playing Outside in Their Neighborhoods

	FIFTH GRADE	EIGHTH GRADE	COMBINED
TOTAL	**16%**	**9%**	**12%**
Boys	12	7	10
Girls	20	10	15
Urban	21	11	17
Suburban	13	8	10
Rural/small town	16	9	12

SOURCE: The Carnegie Foundation for the Advancement of Teaching, Survey of Fifth- and Eighth-Graders, 1988.

gained in economic productivity but compromised their ability to meet humankind's deepest yearning—the longing for social bonds and shared meaning.[2] After speaking with teachers, parents, and children, we concluded that this is precisely what's happening in America today. Vacant lots are gone or filled with debris, cars jam the streets, sidewalks are crowded. There is a rising tide of violence. And children suffer most.

During school visits we asked youngsters to describe their neighborhoods. A young boy in a big midwestern city said, "It's bad. They shoot any time. When you get out of school, they shoot. I stay in the house." An eighth-grader from rural New Mexico told us: "You don't know if somebody is going to go to our house and do something—while I'm there by myself and stuff." Another eighth-grader reported: "I'm often scared going back and forth to school. Kids are after me. I'll fight if I have to" (table 12).

When Carnegie researchers surveyed fifth- and eighth-graders several years ago, more than half agreed that "there are *not* a lot of good places to play in this neighborhood" (table 13). One out of five said drugs are a problem. In another national survey of children, over half reported that they had been "bothered" by an older person while playing out-

Table 13

Children Reporting That There Are Many
Good Places to Play in Their Neighborhoods

	FIFTH GRADE	EIGHTH GRADE	COMBINED
TOTAL	**59%**	**45%**	**52%**
Boys	63	49	56
Girls	55	42	48
Urban	56	45	50
Suburban	61	47	54
Rural/small town	62	44	53

SOURCE: The Carnegie Foundation for the Advancement of Teaching, Survey of Fifth- and Eighth-Graders, 1988.

side. In no community—city, suburb, town, or country—did a majority say their neighborhood was "very good."[3] A kindergarten teacher in Madison, Wisconsin, responding to our survey, said, "Many of my children come to school worried about the violent events they've experienced in their neighborhoods."

The growth of suburbia that followed the Second World War was supposed to be a boon to children, freeing them from the crime and congestion of the city. But suburbs, often without sidewalks, isolated children and made it more difficult for them to walk to school, or even to a friend's house. Mothers became chauffeurs, hauling youngsters off to Little League or to the dentist, whizzing right past neighbors. One suburban mother said, "My nine-year-old has no friends in walking distance, so he has to be chauffeured to all play dates."[4]

Gwendolyn Wright, an urban planning expert, described recent housing developments as a search for "some middle ground between suburban sprawl and urban high-rise, between isolation in the suburbs and anonymity in the cities."[5] Townhouses have become popular, with common grounds for recreation—tennis courts, walking paths, pools—spaces in which a sense of neighborhood could grow. But again, the emphasis is on adults, not children. Battery Park City, a huge complex on the southern tip of Manhattan, was conceived as an inspirational setting for its residents, but children were forgotten. There was little play space, and it was difficult to get to a day-care center. Belatedly, a handful of parents pushed for recreational and gardening space to make this "future city" more child-friendly.[6]

It's bad enough when planners ignore children; it's even worse when they exclude them altogether. According to a nationwide study, in the past an astounding 76 percent of the rental apartments in this country had exclusionary policies with respect to families with children.[7] Moreover, a number of planned communities were designed "for adults only." In Houston, for example, one developer erected a wall to mark the boundary of a child-free ghetto.[8] Such restrictions, for the most part, are now illegal; however, hostility toward children persists.

The time has come to revive our neighborhoods, to create safe places for play and learning in every community. The simple days are gone, of course, the times when children played in the streets, yielding grudgingly to a passing "horseless carriage." Yet, surely we can reconstruct decaying neighborhoods to make them more suitable for children, more welcoming. When new residential and commercial developments are being planned, for example, why can't children's interests be more vigorously represented? Specifically, we urge that all developers prepare a "children's impact" statement for every major project. After all, codes now require developers to meet environmental standards. Why not require "children's standards"?

At their best, neighborhoods provide opportunities for exploration, places where children can extend their knowledge of the world, and parks and playgrounds for exercise and play. When youngsters were asked how their neighborhoods could be improved, the most frequent response was "better places to play." Further, in a survey of parents, 24 percent said that their community did *not* have suitable facilities for children. An additional 18 percent described their local parks or playgrounds as "not very good," or "not good at all."[9]

94

Many playgrounds have become asphalt afterthoughts, built more for the convenience of maintenance workers than for kids. They are surfaced with blacktop, surrounded by chain link fences, with play equipment bolted down. After a few slides and swing rides, there's not much left to do. Children much prefer informal spaces, full of wildlife and trees, places where they can hide or climb or find seclusion.[10] When adults were asked to recall their own favorite childhood environments, they most often thought of empty lots, or woods, or even city streets—less often of playgrounds.[11]

Many countries have constructed parks for creative play and learning. The Scandinavians, for example, have well-supervised "adventure playgrounds," spaces with tree houses, towers to climb, rope swings, ponds for wading, gardens, objects to collect—perfect places for free play *and* environmental education. Children work and play independently, planning their own projects, using materials that lie around.[12] In Tokyo, the Hanuka Adventure Play Park—a spectacular space for children—has an enormous mud slope with running water, a wonderfully inviting place where preschoolers spend hours building dams, channels, and mud structures.

In Germany, "youth farms," usually designed for older children, feature a wide variety of activities—playing music, fire-building, rearing livestock, horseback riding. Something called the "urban farm" is particularly successful in Great Britain. Here the emphasis is on community gardening for all age groups. Children do more than pull weeds. They help plan the garden space, making it their own.[13] Toronto has an adventure playground and Ruth Velk, the supervisor, said: "When the kids come in here, they don't need language. You just see these sparkling eyes and they transform. We have kids coming in here who are at each other's throats all week, but here they figure out how to cooperate, to build something together. There's something magical about it."

Here at home, artists in North Philadelphia turned a vacant inner-city lot into a community art park called "The Village of Arts and Humanities." In the Village, children as young as three create sculptures and murals, and, according to artist Lily Yeh, "The Village" stirred a new sense of community in the neighborhood. The city of Evanston, Illinois, purchased property over the years within its restricted boundaries to create play spaces for young children. Some parcels were very small—no more than one-half or one-quarter of an acre. The result: a network of "Tot Lots" spread across the city.

In New York City's East Harlem, artist Brookie Maxwell organized children and volunteers to reclaim a block-long vacant lot next to a one-hundred-foot blank wall. After clearing three tons of garbage from the lot, the children painted a huge mural on the wall entitled "Dream Street/Calle de Sueños." Maxwell's instructions were to paint a city with "no guns, no violence, no drugs." Some children had great difficulty imagining such a place; one boy burst into tears. The children persevered. The result is a poignant display of dreams, a street-scene mural where children play without fear, where grass grows high, and trees sprout from buildings in an urban landscape. The nonprofit organization Maxwell founded, Creative Arts Workshops, continues to sponsor and organize ambitious art projects to give the most at-risk city children creative outlets and a sense of belonging and of making a positive difference in their neighborhoods.[14]

Playgrounds designed by Robert Leathers & Associates of Ithaca, New York, are built by neighborhoods. Parents and children meet with designers, suggesting play structures they'd like. More than six hundred "Leathers playgrounds" have been built throughout the country, each one-of-a-kind, designed to stimulate a child's imagination, muscle development, and motor skills. Frequently, the playground includes rockets, trampolines, bridges, towers, slides, crawl spaces, and structures for handicapped kids. Recently, citizens in Rockford, Illinois, put together their own outdoor hands-on science park with a cave, suspension bridges, echo machines, a weather station, and "whisper dishes" that let children communicate over a two-hundred-foot distance.

In Kingston, New York, Kimberly Kross, a mother of three "very active boys," said she found no creative play space in city parks. In response, she volunteered to initiate the building of a new Leathers playground. "Kinderland" was the result. It includes a castle, tree fort, mirror maze, trolley rides, and swings. In an amphitheater at the center, parents watch their children and chat with other parents. A slide deposits children right into the middle of a sandpile. A tall "Dinobumpy" slide is a favorite, along with the balance beams, rings, and climbing spaces. Kinderland attracts seventy-five to one hundred preschoolers daily. One mother drives thirty-five miles so her child can play there.

When it comes to creating neighborhoods for children, *indoor* spaces—unused commercial centers and warehouses—should not be overlooked. Consider, for example, that in 1991, 22 percent of the commercial space in this country stood vacant. Manhattan alone has more than fifty million square feet of empty space.[15] Couldn't some of this be converted into a network of "indoor parks," scattered in neighborhoods all around the city?

In downtown Raleigh, North Carolina, a former commercial building has become an indoor park with places to climb and "activity zones" for imaginary play. There is a child-size grocery store, a hospital emergency room, and a big sandpile. This park is exclusively for youngsters up to age seven—a place where, for a small fee, children and parents come for fun and learning. The mother of one preschooler described Raleigh's indoor park as "wonderful for my three-year-old daughter who is handicapped. The play area has a series of 'mills' and 'falls' and Sara just loves being there!" Robin Moore, one of the designers, has proposed that similar "safe havens" be built throughout the country. Indeed, why not challenge students in architecture schools to design creative "indoor parks" for our children as a senior-year project?

Evendale, Ohio, has an indoor center for all ages, with pool and table tennis and video games, a sand volleyball court, rooms for toddlers with child-sized wash basins and drinking fountains. A playground for preschoolers includes a "tricycle track."[16] The physical development of children is so much a part of school readiness, and spaces and places for creative play are needed if the first education goal is to be successful.

City rooftops offer lots of possibilities for children—more sun, less carbon monoxide, more safety. In Tokyo, where space is at such a premium, high-rise department stores have rooftop playgrounds for customers and their children. The Hermann Hospital in Houston, Texas, has a rooftop playground for pediatric patients. Recently, the Lyceum Kennedy, a private school in New York City, built a playground atop a ninety-nine-year-old building in the heart of Manhattan. At first, nearby workers, whose offices overlooked the playground, worried that laughter and noisy chatter would disturb them. As it turned out, the sounds were "soothing and undistracting," said one nearby worker. "Playground sounds, we noticed only this morning, have a way of scurrying up the wall, tapping on the window, settling in right next to you."[17] Why not build a network of "playgrounds in the sky" in every city?

With imaginative planning—and lots of courage—even city streets could be transformed into a network of street parks in densely populated neighborhoods. But for this to happen, we must become at least as concerned about kids as we are about cars.

There was a day when streets were great places for stickball, hopscotch, and sledding in the winter. A kind of standoff existed between children and machines, and youngsters would reluctantly move aside when the carriage, then the car, came along. But with the explosion of traffic, not only play, but life itself was threatened. Between 1910 and 1913, over 40 percent of New York City traffic victims were under the age of fifteen. By 1914, the proportion grew to 60 percent. Most of the accidents took place just a block or two from the victim's home. In response, "Save the Children's Lives" committees sprang up. Rallies were held. Reformers campaigned for child safety laws. Street games were outlawed, playgrounds constructed, and children were arrested for playing in the street, or even for "making noise." By 1930, the number of child deaths from street accidents had dramatically declined. But so had play possibilities for children.[18]

98

No one imagines reclaiming every street. Still, is it unreasonable to hope that, even in our busiest cities, streets *selectively* could be closed off, creating instant street-parks, with good lighting and supervision? The Dutch have, in fact, cut off many through-streets, turning them into cul-de-sacs called *woonerven*. In these protective spaces, intimate neighborhoods have formed. Children play in safety. Small gardens and trees have been planted. Local residents, once again, feel safe.[19] We urge that in cities here at home "street parks" be established in urban areas, making spaces for creative play available to children *right now*.

On a more modest scale, streets might be cordoned off temporarily, for several weeks, especially in the summer. The New York City Police Athletic League has, for years, created such parks. A few years ago, 110 blocks were closed off. Fire hydrants were opened, spouting cascades of cool water. Children frolicked, and recreation staff joined in playful games. Even swimming pools on flatbed trucks were wheeled in. Couldn't all cities close off even a few streets for the children?

Putting it all together, we strongly recommend that every community, as a high priority, develop a "master plan for play," identifying—neighborhood by neighborhood—all of the possible spaces and places for children, building a network of outdoor and indoor parks to provide opportunities for exercise, exploration, and learning.

Children need safe streets and better parks. But children also need lots of "learning stations" in their neighborhoods—libraries, museums, and zoos, for example—which are at the very heart of a school-readiness program. Each one of these child-centered institutions should be well supported by the community, have active preschool programs, and be used frequently by families. And yet, a recent survey revealed that only about one-third of today's parents often take their children to visit a library (figure 11).[20] Even for college graduates the percentage is only 53 percent. Equally disturbing, only about one parent in five says that they visit an art gallery, museum, or historical site with their children.

99

Figure 11

Three- to Five-Year-Olds Whose Parents
Frequently Take Them on Cultural Outings

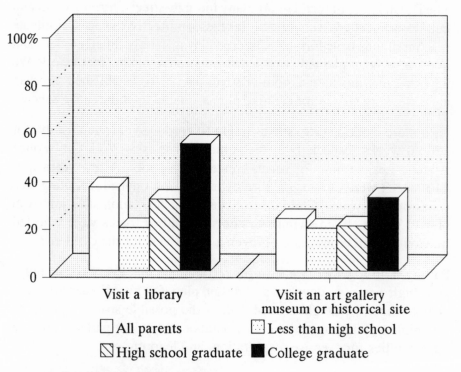

Note: Children enrolled in kindergarten excluded.

Source: National Center for Education Statistics, 1991; in the National Education Goals Panel, *The National Education Goals Report: Building a Nation of Learners* (Washington, DC: National Education Goals Panel, 1991), 37.

Libraries, we believe, have a special role to play in a school-readiness campaign, offering children entry into the world of books, helping them develop language skills, and stirring the imagination. As the director of the Brooklyn Public Library put it, libraries are places "where wonders can be unlocked and new worlds explored."[21]

In the small village of Rocky Hill, New Jersey, as in so many communities, the library has a lively children's center with story hours, children's films, and crafts activities. It's a place where families come together. Just down the road, in Princeton, the public library has a recommended reading series about going off to kindergarten. *Will I Have a Friend?* by Miriam Cohen follows a young boy named Jim through his first day at school, when everyone else except him seems to have found a friend. *Willie Bear* by Mildred Kantrowitz describes a child preparing for the first day of school and leaving his stuffed animals behind. *What I Hear in My School* by June Behrens traces the origin of sounds heard during a school day in the classrooms and on the playground.

Museums are exciting learning centers, too, especially those built exclusively for children. More than four hundred such museums have, in fact, been developed just since the 1970s. All are devoted entirely to exhibitions and programs for youngsters.[22] San Francisco's Exploratorium is a hands-on science museum. The Cleveland Children's Museum sets aside Tuesday mornings specifically for preschoolers so young children can walk around and look at exhibits, manipulating them at their own pace. Boston's Children's Museum is truly a learning center with lots of hands-on exhibits, including one called "Playspace." This museum also conducts workshops on self-esteem and what to expect in school.

Cultural centers serving the general public can also be Ready-to-Learn Centers for preschoolers. The Herbert F. Johnson Museum of Art at Cornell University in Ithaca, New York, has what it calls "bag tours"—canvas bags filled with art materials and books, which are given to preschool teachers and children. The goal: to stimulate young children's creativity in the arts. The "Family Express" program of the Cleveland Museum of Art encourages preschoolers in art, working with their parents. Together they create cut-paper carpets, ceramics, and ink paintings. In Pittsburgh, a unique institution called simply "The Carnegie" has an education department with classes for preschoolers. Children as young as two-and-a-half or three, accompanied by their parents, can enroll in an "Art Express" class or in the natural history museum's "Touch and Tell" program. Beginning at age four, youngsters enroll in science classes that feature computer experience, hands-on science projects, and math puzzles.

101

Ironically, at the very time libraries, museums, galleries, and zoos have such a special role to play, budgets are being slashed, hours restricted, and services cut back. In Massachusetts, for example, twenty branch libraries have been closed, and 30 percent of the remaining libraries have substantially reduced their hours.[23] In the small town of Gray, Maine, the public library has cut services from forty to sixteen hours a week and is only open two days a week. Children's story time has vanished.[24] What's happening to the priorities in this country?

We strongly recommend that communities give priority to the cultural centers that have so much to offer to our children. Every library, museum, and zoo should be well funded and should establish a well-rounded school-readiness program. Municipal authorities should give top priority to the support of such efforts.

Schools surely can be Ready-to-Learn Centers, too, by offering "after-hours" programs for preschoolers or even converting their own hard-surface playgrounds into inviting spaces. At the Ossington-Old Orchard School in Toronto, parents convinced school officials to tear up the asphalt playground and plant trees, flowers, and vegetables in the space. Today the park includes an aviary that attracts wild birds and a hillside that replicates a native Canadian forest. Every summer morning, preschoolers go into the vegetable garden and harvest food, sometimes for their own lunches. It's a place where people of all ages meet. Senior citizens help youngsters with gardening. Older students work with three- and four-year-olds, helping them pick peas and catch tomato bugs.

One of the most neglected possibilities for learning are shops and stores. The shopping mall, for example, has become the modern-day equivalent of the village green—a place where families gather, not only to shop, but also to relax and browse. But what does a child learn? The escalators, fast-food emporiums, pet shops, card stores, and noisy "video game centers" offer little of value to young children. Still, the potential is enormous. We therefore recommend that every major shopping mall include a Ready-to-Learn Center. What we imagine is a "learning zone" filled with toys, books, jungle gyms, big building blocks, and educational videos—an inviting, creative space where children engage in educative play.

The Sutter Square Galleria in downtown Sacramento, California, has a center called "Visionarium," that includes exhibitions where children can learn, guided by staff. Youngsters create "bubble structures" with lots of shapes and patterns. At another, they use raceways and golf balls on inclined surfaces to explore the laws of motion. A "light and color" display uses mirrors, prisms, flashlights, and streetlights. "Safety Pals" tells youngsters about helpers in their community—police officers, firefighters, and mail carriers. A "Watch Me Grow" center, built especially for children under three, has a castle, a slide, climbing bars, dress-up clothes and, instead of sand, a "cornmeal" box for creative play. The Visionarium also has a "nursing station" plus a "movie section" where children create their own animated cartoons.

In Naperville, Illinois, McDonald's Corporation has opened "Leaps & Bounds," its first indoor pay-to-play playground, designed for children from infancy to age twelve. Upon entering the eleven-thousand-square-foot play center, parents and children take off their shoes and check them in to a "Sneaker Keeper." They then turn to over forty different play possibilities—"turbo slides," crawl tunnels, five hundred feet of mazes and tubing suspended from the ceiling, and twenty-five thousand colorful plastic balls. A "Ladder Pull" enhances muscular strength and endurance. A "Rope Walk" develops balancing skills along with eye/foot coordination. In a "Turtle Shell," young children learn the concepts of "in and out," "over and around," and "how big. . . ." Activities are organized by age. "It is designed as 'play with purpose,' " said Terry Capatosto at McDonald's. "In the course of what is designed as free play, the activities are actually meant to develop the child's physical and social skills. It encourages families to play together. Parents tell us nowhere else can they play *with* their children. At most playgrounds they stand back and watch."

Discovery Zone, a new national franchise, is building indoor playgrounds in malls and shopping centers with brightly colored "ball baths," human-sized gerbil tunnels, unusual slides, bouncy water beds, moonwalks, a mini-racetrack, and an obstacle course. Children pay based on a sliding scale for one, two, or three hours of play.[25] Dick Guggenheimer, owner of Discovery Zone in Yonkers, New York, told us: "We're indoors, we're padded; parents can feel their child is safe." A Minneapolis "educational mall," scheduled to open in 1992, will include a preschool program or child-care center, an aquarium, and perhaps a miniature golf course. Children will attend classes while their parents work.[26]

Here's the point: All of this is not just play, as important as that is. It is play with a purpose that is surely related to school readiness. "Children love to play," said James Rippe, a cardiologist at the University of Massachusetts Medical School and a specialist on health and fitness. "Childhood play serves a number of purposes. It should be fun, and in the process contribute to the development of their motor, muscular, and cardiovascular fitness. Play time is also a learning time and a great way for parents to communicate and learn with their children, an added important benefit."

Looking around neighborhoods, almost every store or public space is, potentially, a Ready-to-Learn Center. The Danes, for example, have created children's spaces in banks, with child-sized furniture and toys. In Japan, banks hire employees to greet customers and make children feel welcome, giving them books to read while parents do their banking. In Iceland, banks have "pint-sized" teller windows where children bank. The Pittsburgh, Denver, San Jose, and Boston airports now have play spaces, and the Raleigh-Durham airport will soon construct a play space with an air-flight theme, complete with a kid's cockpit.

Why not open up department stores and shops to children, showing them what goes on inside, what's being made, and how it works? Children, in this country, know all about consuming; they are constantly being pressured to buy things in hard-sell commercials. But they're not learning about how things are made, or even what work is all about.

They see their parents go off in the morning and come home at night. But what in the world do grown-ups *do*?

On a Chicago street, violin makers work facing their storefront window so everyone, including neighborhood children, can watch them at work. Children frequently stop by to see the masters practice their craft. Why couldn't almost every kind of store—bakeries, art supply houses, print shops, supermarkets—have an "open window" on its work, offering a special ready-to-learn tour for preschoolers?

The Grand Union food chain has "learning tours" for children, occasions when managers of various departments tell where foods come from, describe how they are processed and packaged, answer questions and, of course, offer samples. On these excursions, children watch fresh orange juice being squeezed, and have a taste. They use a label gun, operate the checkout scanners, and learn about the store's recycling program. They go behind the scenes, learn about the coolers, and see loading docks. Ed Tucker, manager of Grand Union's flagship store in New York, put it simply: "The tours are good for the kids and good for Grand Union, too."

 All Ready-to-Learn Centers in a neighborhood—from libraries to shopping malls—should be well marked, using perhaps a logo signifying a "child-friendly place." Parents driving down the street and seeing such a logo would know that this is a neighborhood for children. In newspaper advertisements, businesses could display ready-to-learn logos, signaling that parents *and* children are welcome. Television stations could use the logo to identify children's programs.

Every community might also prepare a "Ready-to-Learn Directory" to help parents locate businesses with special children's services. Such a booklet could list programs for preschoolers at libraries, parks, and shopping malls. Newspapers could run weekly "Ready-to-Learn Supplements." *The Journal-Gazette* in Fort Wayne, Indiana, for example, has a regular section called "Living for Kids." A recent edition was headlined, ''Have Fun Visiting the Place Where Art Lives''—a story about children's programs at local galleries and museums.

What we imagine, then, are neighborhoods with literally dozens of well-marked, child-friendly spaces and places for learning. But for this to work, *people* will be needed, to supervise and teach. In Denmark and Sweden, a corps of respected professionals called ''social teachers'' work with children in housing co-ops, adventure playgrounds, parks, and afterschool centers, engaged in projects that range from tree planting to theatre productions. In São Paulo, Brazil, the city's children's bureau recently launched a major program. Animators, actors, singers, and dancers, some paid twice as much as teachers, are sent out into the neighborhoods, including the worst slums, to bring the performing arts to children and draw children on the margins into the center of the nation's life.

We propose that a Ready-to-Learn Service Corps be created in this country—with thousands of high school and college students recruited as volunteers in a national campaign. Such volunteers might spend several hours every week reading to children in a library, taking them on a tour of the local bakery, volunteering at a school-readiness center or at the mall, or serving as recreation leaders at a local park. Every school and college in the community could sponsor such a service corps, calling for participation as a graduation requirement, staffing projects in the neighborhood surrounding the institution. Further, the proposed corps could be linked to the National and Community Service Act of 1990, which encourages community service, conservation, and service-learning programs in schools and colleges.

Last year at Michigan State University, student residence halls sponsored Halloween programs and the College of Agriculture organized an Animal Day for preschoolers. Princeton University students work with preschoolers through the Young Mother Outreach Program. Women students are ''big sisters'' to teenage mothers and their babies at the Union Industrial Home for Children in nearby Trenton. Texas Woman's University converted a student residence hall into apartments for single mothers and their children. While the mothers work and go to class,

106

their youngsters are cared for by college students. Volunteer workers such as these can serve in every community in the country.

The time has come for America to reclaim its neighborhoods for children. Each community should be a safe and inviting place with opportunities for creative play and growth. Fred Rogers of "Mister Rogers' Neighborhood" put the challenge this way: "Everything [we do must be] done . . . to encourage children to feel good about who they are, to help them understand themselves and their world, to enhance their healthy curiosity about that world, and to support in them an optimistic striving toward what they can become."[27] If all children in America are to be ready for school, we must have neighborhoods for learning.

CONNECTIONS ACROSS THE GENERATIONS

"THE CONTINUITY OF ALL CULTURES depends on the living presence of at least three generations," wrote anthropologist Margaret Mead.[1] Older people are inspired by the innocence and hopefulness of the young, while children, through close and cordial involvement with their elders, discover roots and gain confidence to make their way through life. Preschoolers, in particular, need such connections to extend knowledge, deepen social confidence, enrich language skills, and develop a sense of moral awareness, increasing their capacity to learn.

A child's school readiness is enhanced by connections across generations. We propose, therefore, that new intergenerational institutions be built, with day-care centers and retirement villages combining programs, for example. We suggest, as well, "Grandteacher" programs that bring older people into child-care centers and preschools as tutors and mentors. We urge that a host of institutions—libraries, schools, churches—sponsor intergenerational projects and finally, we suggest that entire communities schedule "Grand Days" to bring the old and young together.

The movie "Avalon," which traces the lives of a Baltimore immigrant family for three generations, features a touching relationship between a grandfather and grandson. Grandson Michael was someone grandfather could tell his stories to, passing on his wisdom, sharing memories. Grandfather, on the other hand, became Michael's special friend, someone in whom he could confide. In the intimacy of this bond, the youngster was learning and stretching while Grandfather was sharing and teaching—passing on traditions.

Table 14

Family Issues of Concern to Fifth-Graders

	PERCENTAGE AGREEING
When I come home from school, there is usually an adult there to meet me	70%
I would like to spend more time with my mother	59
I would like to spend more time with my father	54
I would like to spend more time with my grandparents	39

SOURCE: The Carnegie Foundation for the Advancement of Teaching, Survey of Fifth- and Eighth-Graders, 1988.

Today, such close-knit relationships are fast fading. John Gatto, recently New York City's Teacher of the Year, vividly describes the growing sense of alienation that seems to be separating the generations. "We live in a time of great social crisis," he said. "We seem to have lost our identity. Children and old people are penned up and locked away from the business of the world to a degree without precedent; nobody talks to them anymore. Without children and old people mixing in daily life, a community has no future and no past, only a continuous present. In fact, the word *community* hardly applies to the way we interact with each other. We live in networks, not communities, and everyone I know is lonely because of that."[2]

This loss of community, this social fragmentation, while threatening to everyone, is most damaging to children. According to a Carnegie Foundation survey, 30 percent of the nation's fifth-graders go home every afternoon to an empty house. Almost 60 percent would like to spend more time with their mother. More than half wish they could be with their father more and nearly 40 percent want more time with grandparents (table 14). "I'm always alone," a young student told us. "I don't have any sisters or brothers, and my parents always go out with their own friends and leave me by myself. And at home, there's nothing to do. I feel really lonely.'' What about older people in the neighborhood? ''We just never meet,'' said one youngster. ''They sort of live in a separate world.''

An older person can give children perspective on the past and a vision of the future, offering them rich experiences filled with lessons of life. Intergenerational connections provide security, a sense of continuity, and a feeling of belonging. Research summarized by the Education Commission of the States put it this way: ''. . . children who come to school capable of trust, initiative, . . . and with a sense of control and purpose to their lives, are far more ready and able to learn than students who lack these psychological basics.''[3] Yet ''it is a modern paradox that children are far more likely to have living grandparents but much less likely to know them well,'' says Fran Pratt of the Center for Understanding Aging at Framingham State College in Massachusetts.[4]

Psychiatrist James Comer, in reflecting on his own childhood, concluded that much of the trouble we attribute to our young really stems from their sense of separation from the larger world. When he was growing up, Comer says, adults were locked into a ''conspiracy'' of protection for a child.[5] ''And children knew what to expect,'' he says. ''Everyone had a real sense of place and belonging. Even if you didn't have a high status, you really had a sense of community. . . . Everything a child knew about what was right and wrong, good and bad, came to him or her through those adult authority figures. Now we may not think of that as so desirable; on the other hand, those young people felt supported by the adults who could sanction or not sanction behavior.''[6]

Without a ''conspiracy of protection,'' today's children are socially, emotionally, and educationally at risk. They are adrift, without a steady moral compass to direct their daily behavior or to plot a thoughtful and responsible course for their lives.[7] ''Children are growing up alone,'' one kindergarten teacher told us, ''and I really think it's sad that they never seem to be with older people. They don't know how adults think or what they do. I'm convinced it affects their learning.'' Another said: ''Children are coming to school with so much confusion about whom to trust. They need continuity and a sense of belonging, and I'd like to see more extended families take responsibility for educating their youth.''

Intergenerational ties begin, of course, at home. In the late nineteenth century, as waves of immigrants moved into America's cities, something called ''the family circle'' brought relatives together to share experiences and discuss, in cordial fashion, everyday family problems.[8] While elders talked, the children played, and all were held together by a thread of kinship. Family-circle pressure could, at times, be oppressive, and relationships were not always harmonious. Still, this large, extended family had a way of breaking tension, giving encouragement and support to children, and strengthening family bonds.

Such intimate family circles may be unrealistic now. Relatives are scattered. Everyone is too busy. Still, we all need roots, and family relationships surely can be reinforced, at least occasionally, by celebrations that bring relatives together. Several years ago, the National Council of Negro Women began hosting family reunions in big-city parks across the country. People came. Whole families gathered to picnic, share food, swap stories, talk about old times. Over the past five years, *four million* people have gathered for these reunions.[9]

Bringing families closer will help. But it is becoming increasingly apparent that the very structure of our modern institutions must also be candidly reexamined. Today, generations exist side by side, brushing elbows, yet hardly touching one another, rarely forging authentic friendships. Even more disturbing, we have actually *institutionalized* this age segregation. Toddlers are in day care, older children are in school, young adults go off to college, parents are in the workplace, older people are in retirement villages, nursing homes, or apartments, living all alone. What we are left with is a ''horizontal culture,'' one in which each age group is disconnected from the others, separated so completely that it is possible, quite literally, to go through life from birth to death, and spend most waking hours only with one's peers.

Intergenerational separation brings discontinuity to the culture and diminishes the school readiness of children who are denied security and

112

perspective. If children are to grow up in a more supportive world, if they are to experience a sense of wholeness, we must overcome the institutional isolation that keeps the separate age groups from interacting with each other. More than sixty years ago, John Dewey said: "Whatever the future may have in store, one thing is certain. Unless local communal life can be restored, the public cannot adequately resolve its most urgent problem, to find and identify itself."[10]

Clearly, the time has come to break up the age ghettos. It is time to create new intergenerational arrangements. Let's begin to arrange our culture "vertically." Let's have institutions that bring the old and young together, with facilities and programs that intersect. Retirement villages and day-care centers, for example, could be organized as a single institution, with overlapping functions. In addition, grandparents could be helpers in preschools, and college campuses could be places where retirees and preschool children come together, too.

Messiah Village, atop one of the rolling hills in Mechanicsburg, Pennsylvania, is one place that brings the old and young together. Tucked beneath the chapel in the main building of this retirement village is a Children's Family Center where 75 youngsters, ages two to five, arrive each day for child care. Breakfast is prepared by one of the village residents known as "Grandma." Other retirees organize games, strawberry festivals, and art classes. They tell stories and help with meals, snacks, and song time. Children walk through the halls almost every day, greeting residents, occasionally joining them in crafts or cooking classes, in exercise sessions, or on strolls along nature trails. The generations also meet for picnics and holiday celebrations. A Special Friends program matches a child with a retiree. Special Friends meet weekly to play games, work puzzles, read, and talk. In such encounters, children learn about growing older, while older people are inspired by the freshness and energy of children. Director Sue Shupp observed: "From my point of view, it can be nothing but good to get the generations back together."

Bringing generations together can occur almost anywhere—schools, day-care centers, and retirement villages. Even the workplace can find a way to build bridges across the generations. In 1990, the Stride Rite

Corporation in Cambridge, Massachusetts, became the first private company in the country to establish an intergenerational day-care center in which preschoolers joined retirees to engage in creative play, paint murals, bake cookies, read stories, dance, and sing. Arnold Hiatt, chairman of Stride Rite, says: "I began thinking about the enormous waste of energy that was building among the retired community, people who didn't have anywhere to channel their energy. I was aware of the opportunities that children provide as a focus. . . . It seemed to me that these two groups had something to give each other."[11]

On quite another front, the Public Library in Los Angeles has a "Grandparents and Books" project in thirty of its branches.[12] Currently, two hundred senior volunteers come to local libraries to read to children and give them a "grandlap." Volunteers make a six-month commitment, agreeing to read at least two hours every week. In a Hispanic neighborhood, where the program was pioneered, one of the first "grandparents" is still reading to young children after three years.

In a program called Family Friends, the National Council on the Aging builds bridges across three generations. A senior citizen becomes "grandparent" to a child, and "parent" to the mother and father. Each volunteer makes a nine-month commitment to visit his or her adopted family at least once a week, while receiving a small stipend to cover supplies, meals, and transportation. One mother whose children were assigned a Family Friend commented: "My boys have a wonderful, new, wise, and loving friend to learn from and look up to. In addition, I have a trusted and reliable companion to lean on, who helps ease the everyday difficulties."[13]

Churches, synagogues, and mosques also have a special role to play. Traditionally, worship has been an occasion when family members joined in a shared experience. Recently, however, some church groups have organized almost all social and even religious functions by age. Toddlers, singles, teenagers, retirees gather in the same building, but rarely meet. Organizing social activities according to age makes sense. But religious celebrations and even socials can also have a communal function that strengthens families and gives a sense of purpose across generations. We urge, therefore, that all religious institutions give special attention to intergenerational efforts through worship, social hours, and sponsored projects.

Hearts and Hands at the First United Methodist Church in Topeka, Kansas, involves the old and young. Seniors in the congregation sit with the two- to five-year-olds at the day-care center as they nap, allowing regular caregivers to conduct staff meetings. Other seniors make doll clothes, do grocery shopping, and build playground equipment and storage sheds for toys. Several volunteers constructed a stage for the children's plays. Entire families participate in monthly birthday celebrations—singing, playing games, enjoying each other's company. An elderly person confined to a wheelchair reads to the children, tells stories, and answers questions. Teacher Kathie Price told us: "We didn't know how the kids would react to a disabled person, but they took to her immediately. Kids have a lot less trouble accepting older people than the rest of us."

The Charles E. Smith Jewish Day School in Rockville, Maryland, has a pen-pal program with Revitz House, a nearby Jewish retirement community. Little children are paired with retirees. They write letters throughout the school year, describing themselves and asking their correspondents to do the same. One elderly woman wrote this simple message: "When I was a girl I had brown hair like you, but now my hair has turned gray," capturing perfectly the intergenerational message. Children visit the retirement village to meet their pen pals, and parents often accompany them on trips. Holiday celebrations are shared, and friendships occasionally are sustained as the children grow older. Teacher Susan Bonnett, who started the program, integrates the day-care curriculum around an intergenerational theme, using books like *Mandy's Grandmother* by Liesel Moak Skorpen or *Kevin's Grandma* by Barbara Williams.

Beyond informal contacts such as these, older people can become actively involved in the actual work of day-care centers, preschools, and even participate in home-service. We specifically recommend that a "Grandteacher Program" be created in communities all across the

115

country, which would, we believe, be helpful to both age groups. It is an activity psychologist Erik Erikson refers to as "generativity"— older people being concerned about the coming generation in a larger, more communal sense. Adults who lack such concern, Erikson says, will stagnate, lose hope.[14] But it works both ways. When senior citizens worked in child-care programs in three cities—Memphis, San Francisco, and Pittsburgh—teachers reported that children were more motivated to learn and more cooperative as a result of the experience.[15]

Sally Newman, director of Generations Together at the University of Pittsburgh, notes that senior citizens can be especially helpful in the growing child-care field, not only providing extra help, but most important, adding quality as well.[16] According to a University of Pittsburgh study, 60 percent of mothers enrolling their infants and preschoolers in day care want mature child-care providers.[17] As one kindergarten teacher suggested: "Many of us are so busy that there's no time to just visit with the children—or just *listen*. It would be great to have a spare grandma or grandpa. They could listen to the children's concerns, and even share their dreams."

The good news is that such connections are taking place. Today, 25 percent of family day-care workers, 13 percent of the staff in child-care centers, and 7 percent of preschool teachers are seniors, over the age of 55.[18] At Point Park Children's School, in Pittsburgh, senior citizens work in a center that includes infants, toddlers, and preschoolers. Director Betty Lisowski told us: "Lots of the kids have no grandparents, and these older people provide for a much richer life for children, things you can't learn from a book. It's sort of like folklore, different life experiences passed along, even for these youngest children." She is quick to praise the one hundred hours of training these "olders" have received and emphasizes the positive influence they have on the younger staff. "Lots of child-care workers are extremely young themselves—right out of school," she said. "It's good for them to see the strong work ethic of this generation where work is taken much more seriously. It's good for the younger staff to have that kind of ethical code as a model."

116

The Center for Intergenerational Learning at Temple University has a program called ECHO—Elders and Children Helping Each Other—in which retirees are trained to work in preschool programs. Director Nancy Henkin says the goal is to give elders "confidence to realize they can make a difference in the lives of children, and offers children models." One elder participant, who doesn't have a family of her own nearby, works at a child-care center at the local Naval Yard. She is in charge of crafts, which, she says, "has given me an exciting new interest."[19]

In San Francisco, thirty-five children, ages two to six, are cared for by elders from sunup to sundown at the Sunshine Garden School. The older people received special training and receive modest stipends. At the University of North Carolina's Senior Academy for Intergenerational Learning in Asheville, retirees teach children in the preschools. One participant noted: "You don't see many people around here looking for something to do."

Foster Grandparents is a federally funded program in which low-income seniors become companions to disadvantaged children. Typically, such grandparents, paid a modest stipend, work several hours with two children a day, in the child's home, in a hospital, or another institution. Often they become "real" grandparents, heaping love on them, talking with them, coming to care about them deeply. With so many older Americans yearning to give, with hundreds of thousands of children aching for just a touch of love, what could be more logical? This is a chance for old and young Americans to answer each other's needs and to get to know each other. Clarence Young, a Foster Grandparent in Louisville, Kentucky, was asked to work with cerebral palsy youngsters. "It was wonderfully satisfactory," he said, "to help these children and watch them learn to do things for themselves that they were not formerly able to do."

Older citizens can also help fill in the two- to three-hour gap between the end of preschool and the end of the workday. Right now, many parents are frustrated because no service is available after preschool. They can't leave work, there is no one at home or in the neighborhood

117

to call on for help, and yet it's just not possible to move the preschoolers from one location to another. In response to this special crisis, we suggest that older citizens be available to teach crafts, read stories or provide laptime in the late afternoon. Volunteers might work several days a week, or possibly one week every month.

AgeLink, an intergenerational program run by Western Carolina University, uses retirees from the region where there is a reservoir of talent waiting to be tapped. One hundred retirees participate in a program that offers after-hours services to six hundred children, many from single-parent homes. Some retirees help in the homes of licensed care providers. Others care for children in the preschool, taking them on trips in the afternoon or becoming a "phone friend." Retirees who spend time with young children in programs such as this should give love, of course. But the focus can be on language and learning, too. Consider, for example, the great opportunity older people have to tell exciting stories about "when I was growing up." Such conversations give children living history and promote school readiness and special bonding.

Former surgeon general C. Everett Koop, recalling his childhood in Brooklyn, described just how enriching intergenerational relationships can be. "Like many youngsters in those days," he said, "it was my privilege to grow up in a three-generation world. I am saddened to read that today only 9 percent of children in the United States live within walking distance of their grandparents. . . . As a child, I reveled in being surrounded by a large family. Five backyards down Fifteenth Street, I could see the house of my maternal grandfather, Grandpa Apel, . . . (who) taught me the special responsibility and pleasure of being generous, not only with money, but also with time. . . . We talked constantly. I knew everything about his German childhood. . . . I lived and relived his becalmed six-week crossing of the Atlantic on a sailing vessel so that I could almost feel the hunger pangs from the weeks without food. . . . Most important, I saw things and people through his eyes."[20]

Finally, "Connections Across the Generations" is a theme around which an entire community might rally. Cities, towns, and villages

118

could sponsor "Grand Picnics" in which older people and preschoolers come together. Merchants could sponsor "Grand Shopping Trips," giving discounts to intergenerational teams. Travel agents could plan "Grand Travel," catering to grandparents and grandchildren. "Grand-travel" is, in fact, the name of a Chevy Chase, Maryland, tour company that creates domestic and international itineraries to "expand the world of grandparent/grandchildren relationships."[21]

On a more modest scale, communities might plan "Grand Saturdays" or "Grand Weekends," times when senior citizens and little children take short trips together, visiting local sites. To celebrate the national "Grandparent Day" each September, schools and preschools might invite grandparents—both real and adopted—to visit, tell stories, and share a meal. Young families living far away from relatives might form networks with adopted grandparents, building connections across generations.

Dobbs Ferry, New York, has its own special Grandparents Day. Ray Gerson, superintendent of schools, said, "We feel the seniors are part of the community and that the schools are theirs."[22] In nearby Yorktown, a consortium of community groups developed a project called "Roots" in which children interview their grandparents or seniors at local centers about their lives. Louise Corwin, who started the activity, said: "I grew up in a small community in Pennsylvania. There was more cohesion there than I see in some of the communities here. I could go after school and visit both sets of grandparents."[23] We recommend that every community organize a series of intergenerational projects—called perhaps "Grand Days"—in which senior citizens engage in activities and excursions with young children. The possibilities—as well as educational benefits—are almost endless.

Throughout this chapter, we have highlighted the value of grandchildren and grandparents getting close together, underscoring just how much they have to learn from one another. But what we are really concerned about is building a more cohesive and more supportive cultural climate for our littlest children. And this can be achieved by *all* age groups, even high school and college students. Further, as young people have close relationships with little children, they will perhaps become better parents and form intergenerational bonds as they grow older.

At South Brunswick High School in New Jersey, students receive credit for working with preschoolers in activities including recreation and reading. In Kansas City, Missouri, Youth Volunteers work in preschools and in a nursery school for handicapped children. They read to them, talk to them, share their special interests and knowledge, and assist teachers. Middle-school students in Columbia, South Carolina, are busy reaching out, "adopting" preschool children in a housing project. The students read, bake, shop, and play with their younger friends.

At the Child Development Center in Buckhannon, West Virginia, on the campus of West Virginia Wesleyan College, about sixty-five students spend more than fifteen hundred hours at the Center, working with preschoolers. Kay Klausewitz, the director, observed that "the college students are wonderful at interacting with children and give them precisely the socialization and language structures that they need. Students, on the other hand, often discover little children for the first time . . . and become prepared, themselves, to be much better parents." Amherst College students in Massachusetts care for children while their mothers and fathers attend Parents Anonymous meetings. Students at other times visit the families, interacting with the children, helping with cooking and cleaning, creating, in fact, an informal extended family.

We face in this country a growing gap between old and young. Some senior citizens have organized to protect their own special interests, often to the detriment of children. But this country cannot allow itself to be divided. The time has come to affirm a deeper truth: The old and the young truly are dependent on each other. Rachel Carson wrote: "If a child is to keep alive his inborn sense of wonder . . . he needs the companionship of at least one adult who can share it, rediscovering with him the joy, excitement, and mystery of the world we live in."[24]

In the end, intergenerational connections may be the *real* key to quality in education. After all, a ready-to-learn campaign is not just about schools, or even about children. It's about building in this country a new network of support, creating a true community of caring for the coming generation. And all of the steps discussed in this report—from a healthy start to connections across the generations—are bound together by the conviction that, if the future of the nation is to be secure, we must all come together on behalf of children.

A Committed Nation

A COMMITTED NATION

WOVEN THROUGHOUT THIS REPORT is the conviction that we must organize a national effort on behalf of children, looking at the whole of our society. We must acknowledge the interrelatedness of the home, health clinics, preschools, the workplace, television, neighborhoods, and connections across the generations—all of the institutions that influence the lives of children. The time has come to launch a Ready-to-Learn Campaign, one that builds on existing projects, starts new ones where needed, and makes sure all the pieces fit together.

In traveling around the country, we have seen literally hundreds of excellent programs for preschoolers, creative activities that enrich their lives. The problem is that the current effort is so fragmented, and so many children are left behind. Daniel Yankelovich, in discussing America's social dislocations, says that what America now needs is ''a new social ethic. . . . We need new rules to define the epochal tasks that must be accomplished in our era to bring about that minimal harmony between individual and society that is the mark of a successful civilization.''[1]

Ready to Learn is, we believe, one such ''epochal task,'' a cause around which everyone can rally. For the first time in our history the President and governors from all fifty states have defined a goal of transcendent national importance, one concerned not just with the quality of schools but, in the larger sense, with the future of the nation. But how is school readiness for all to be achieved? In a country as decentralized as ours, is it possible to organize a national campaign so that the whole of the effort is greater than the separate parts?

As an initial step, we urge that the President and Congress spell out precisely the role the federal government will play during the decade of the nineties. How can Americans be asked to support a ready-to-learn effort without leadership at the top? Certainly, the federal budget is tight and other priorities must be met. Still, the first education goal is, perhaps more than any other, inextricably linked to the nation's civic, social, and economic well-being. Would it be possible, for example, for leaders in Washington to announce a timetable for the full funding of Head Start? Could we hear a clear plan detailing just when WIC—the nutrition program for women, infants, and children—will be fully funded? And when will basic health care for all poor mothers and babies be delivered? Decisive action is required now.

At the state level, governors should take the lead in launching and co-ordinating the Ready-to-Learn Campaign. Specifically, we suggest that every governor bring into his or her office a school-readiness coordi-nator, someone to help integrate all preschool efforts, coordinating the budgets of health, education, and child services. We'd also like to see each state establish a decade-long ready-to-learn strategy, with timeta-bles for implementing such projects as parent education, preschool pro-grams, family-friendly workplace policies and, of course, better health for children. Finally, every state might schedule an annual ready-to-learn celebration, hosted by the governor, to honor outstanding accompli-shments on behalf of children.

In the end, the Ready-to-Learn Campaign is a local effort. It's in cities, towns, and villages, and in homes, where the action must occur. Every community might, we suggest, organize a Ready-to-Learn Council to coordinate the program. Just as a local school board looks after educa-tion, so the proposed Council should focus on needs of preschool chil-dren. The Council—acting as a voice for children—would integrate the work of separate agencies, take inventory of existing programs to find out what new services might be needed, and build a solid, comprehen-sive Ready-to-Learn Campaign at the local level. Members of the Council could be selected from health and social-service organizations, the recreation department, libraries, parent groups, churches and syna-gogues—and certainly the schools.

We also urge that local Ready-to-Learn Councils develop a yardstick to measure the commitment to young children and prepare, periodically,

126

a report card on how the community is doing. The Council might use for assessment the seven ready-to-learn steps proposed in our report. Here are some possible questions to be considered:

- *Health:* How many of the community's mothers have adequate prenatal care? What is the percentage of low birthweight babies in the area? How many children receive the full range of immunizations? Are there Ready-to-Learn Clinics in the community to provide nutrition and child care, linking health and education?

- *Parents:* Are parents reading to their children? Are there literacy programs available for parents who cannot read? Do all schools offer preschool parent education? Is a Ready-to-Learn Parent Guide available? Have preschool PTAs been formed in each community?

- *Preschool:* Do local Head Start programs reach all eligible children? Do all of the three- and four-year-olds have access to a preschool program? Are local schools working closely with Head Start to ensure continuity in learning? Does the community have adequate child-care facilities? Has the state developed adequate standards to ensure the quality of such programs? Does the local community college offer a degree program for preschool professionals?

- *Workplace:* Do employers provide parental leave? Are flexible scheduling and job sharing encouraged at the workplace? Are employees given "parenting days" each year? Is a child-care information and referral service available to workers?

- *Television:* Do local television stations air programs for preschoolers and their parents? Are community groups trained to monitor local stations, seeing to it that they meet the new FCC regulations? Are Ready-to-Learn Television Guides available to parents? Do local libraries and video stores stock high-quality videos for preschoolers?

- *Neighborhoods:* Does the community have outdoor and indoor parks for young children? Are "street playgrounds" needed? Are

127

libraries, museums, and other learning centers adequately funded? And do they offer ready-to-learn programs? Do shopping malls and stores have Ready-to-Learn Centers? Are high school and college students organized to serve as volunteers in neighborhood children's programs?

· *Generations:* Do schools, day-care centers, and retirement villages bring the young and old together? Do day care centers and preschools have Grandteacher programs in which older people participate as mentors to young children? Does the community sponsor Grand Days that encourage intergenerational connections?

School readiness must be a grass-roots effort, engaging homes and neighborhoods, reaching out to children. But who should take the lead in getting communities organized for action?

As one approach, we suggest that the United Way of America help organize Ready-to-Learn Councils—working closely with mayoral offices and other public and private agencies. The United Way, with 2300 chapters, is America's premier volunteer organization. It represents a community's most charitable impulses. Moreover, United Way has already launched a program called "Mobilization for America's Children," a twenty-year commitment to promote learning readiness. The United Way also supports a host of first-rate preschool programs for young children, including Success by 6, which brings together business and government leaders, school officials, and others to ensure that all children are well prepared for school.[2] Clearly, the United Way has a critically important role to play in launching a community-based Ready-to-Learn Campaign.

School leaders can be helpful, too. Recently, the Charlotte-Mecklenburg Board of Education in North Carolina decided to focus not just on schools but on *children*. A coordination of services was required. Mayor Richard Vinroot set the tone when he said: "Education involves more than what happens between 9:00 a.m. and 3:00 p.m. five days a week." In response, the school board organized a Children's Services

Network. The Network, which brings together all of the community agencies concerned with children, will coordinate services, increase support, and prepare a report card on progress. This could be a model for other communities.[3]

Minneapolis has organized "City's Children: 2007," a coordinated effort operating under the auspices of the Youth Coordinating Board. The goal is to integrate all children's activities in the city. Proposed projects include "school readiness centers" in neighborhoods—places for day care, Head Start, kindergarten, and early childhood programs. "These centers would become the access point in every neighborhood for families to connect with services—and with each other—creating a natural support structure for the healthy development of children from birth to age six," says the director, Richard Mammen.[4]

In Seattle, the Junior League and YMCA, working with municipal officials, took the lead in organizing "KidsPlace," a coordinated, city-wide effort to create a better world for children. As a first step, thousands of Seattle children were surveyed to learn what *they* liked and disliked about their communities. Parks, they said, were the city's best asset. Soon after the poll's release, Seattle voters approved a bond issue to renovate play spaces. In another move, Seattle's aquarium built platforms and lowered display windows for the littlest visitors. The city also installed an emergency phone system for young callers.

KidsPlace achievements also include a resource and referral center for child-care services, a committee to ensure that low-income children get good health care, longer hours at recreation centers, flexible parental leave policies for city workers, a new beach along Seattle's revamped waterfront, and a change in zoning laws to permit day care in city dwellings. One of Seattle's crowning achievements each year is "KidsDay"—a week-long festival of events in October—a time when museums, the zoo, performing arts centers, and even the transit system are free and accessible to all families. The purpose is to create a child-friendly atmosphere, letting families know that the city cherishes its children.

In Palm Beach County, Florida, local officials created a special taxing district to support children's programs, administered by an independent government agency called Children's Services Council. After a county-wide survey, the ten-member council identified sixteen priorities—from reducing school dropouts to improving child care. Thus far, nearly sixty children's projects have been launched, including infant nurseries, intervention programs for kids with special needs, and parent support groups. On the West Coast, a recent referendum in San Francisco requires that a portion of property-tax money be used for child care, tutoring, delinquency prevention, job training, health, and social services. Children have become a priority.[5]

Such initiatives illustrate what can and must be done nationwide. But to give overall direction and visibility to the effort, we suggest that a National Ready-to-Learn Center be established. For years, physical fitness has been promoted with the help of a national office. Why not advance the nation's first education goal—fitness for formal learning—in a similar fashion? This new, nongovernmental Center could be guided by an advisory board that brings together a dozen or so of the nation's major associations concerned with children. It would serve as a clearinghouse for all fifty states, monitor progress, and report periodically to the nation.

The proposed Center also could celebrate success, giving Ready-to-Learn Awards to model programs at a White House ceremony, perhaps, honoring projects in children's health, parent education, creative television, family-friendly worksites, neighborhoods for learning, and intergenerational programs—all of the strategies outlined in this report. Finally, we imagine the Center coordinating a ready-to-learn advertising campaign through the National Advertising Council, perhaps, to promote excellence on behalf of children.

The ready-to-learn mandate presents America with an urgent call, a unique opportunity to think—and act—in more integrative ways, forging new social bonds, bringing together disconnected institutions. In our hard-edged, competitive world, such a campaign on behalf of children may seem quixotic. Not only have cultural connections faded, but the very notion of community seems strikingly inapplicable to contemporary life. Absent larger loyalties in this country, we are settling for little loyalties that diminish our national unity, and widen the social separations. There's a growing feeling that the social pathologies we now confront are just too deep to be remedied and that when it comes to our most glaring problems, especially those affecting children, little, if anything, can be done.

But good will runs deep in America. Throughout our history, the citizens of this country have shown their capacity to come together and organize energetically and to great effect when inspired. We have dedicated ourselves to great causes, responding in times of crisis with vigor and an outpouring of concern. We are confident that with the right blend of commitment and imagination, America can come together once again. Every community can, we believe, find creative ways to promote school readiness and develop strategies that will make a difference for the nation—and most especially for children.

At the historic education summit in Charlottesville, Virginia, President Bush declared: "Let no child in America be forgotten or forsaken."[6] When all is said and done, this is what the Ready-to-Learn Campaign is all about.

SUMMARY OF RECOMMENDATIONS

A MANDATE FOR THE NATION

WHAT FOLLOWS is a seven-step strategy to ensure learning readiness for all the nation's children. Taken together, the following recommendations comprise a comprehensive plan aimed at achieving the nation's number one education goal—by the year 2000, all children will come to school "ready to learn." The seven steps are:

1   A Healthy Start
2   Empowered Parents
3   Quality Preschool
4   A Responsive Workplace
5   Television as Teacher
6   Neighborhoods for Learning
7   Connections Across the Generations

Step One

A HEALTHY START

GOOD HEALTH AND GOOD SCHOOLING are inextricably interlocked, and every child, to be ready to learn, must have a healthy birth, be well nourished, and well protected in the early years of life.

· *Today's students are tomorrow's parents; every school district in this country should offer all students a new health course called "The Life Cycle," with study units threaded through every grade.*

· *The federal nutrition program for women, infants, and young children, known as WIC, should be fully funded so that every eligible mother and infant will be served.*

· *A network of neighborhood-based Ready-to-Learn Clinics should be established in every underserved community across the country to ensure access to basic health care for all mothers and preschool children.*

· *The National Health Service Corps should be expanded to ensure that a well-trained health and education team is available to staff the proposed clinics.*

· *Every state should prepare a county-by-county Maternal and Child Health Master Plan to assure that all regions are covered and that existing resources are well used.*

· *Funding for two key federal health programs—Community and Migrant Health Centers and Maternal and Child Health Block Grants—should be significantly increased, with awards made to states that have justified the need based on a master plan.*

Step Two

EMPOWERED PARENTS

THE HOME is the first classroom. Parents are the first and most essential teachers; all children, as a readiness requirement, should live in a secure environment where empowered parents encourage language development.

- *Every child should live in a language-rich environment in which parents speak frequently to their children, listen carefully to their responses, answer questions, and read aloud to them every day.*

- *A new Ready-to-Learn Reading Series, one with recommended books for preschoolers, should be prepared under the leadership of the American Library Association.*

- *A comprehensive parent education program should be established in every state to guarantee that all mothers and fathers of preschool children have access to such a service.*

- *A national Parent Education Guide, focusing on all dimensions of school readiness, should be prepared collaboratively by state departments of education and distributed widely to parents.*

- *Every community should organize a preschool PTA—supported and encouraged by the National Congress of Parents and Teachers—to bring parents of young children together and to build a bridge between home and school.*

Step Three

QUALITY PRESCHOOL

SINCE MANY YOUNG CHILDREN are cared for outside the home, high-quality preschool programs are required that not only provide good care, but also address all dimensions of school readiness.

- *Head Start should be designated by Congress as an entitlement program and be fully funded by 1995 to ensure that every eligible child will be served.*

- *Every school district in the nation should establish a preschool program as an optional service for all three- and four-year-olds not participating in Head Start.*

- *The new federal initiative—the Child Care and Development Block Grants—should be used by states to start new programs that expand the quality of care for small children, especially in disadvantaged communities.*

- *A National Forum on Child-Care Standards should be convened by the National Association for the Education of Young Children. The Forum's recommendations should be adopted by all states, so that by the year 2000 every day-care center in the country is licensed to meet these standards.*

- *Every community college should make it a special priority to establish an associate degree called the Child-Care Professional and also establish a collaborative relationship with local day-care and preschool programs, offering in-service programs for teachers and providers.*

Step Four

A RESPONSIVE WORKPLACE

IF EACH CHILD in America is to come to school ready to learn, we must have workplace policies that are family-friendly, ones that offer child-care services and give parents time to be with their young children.

· *All employers should make at least twelve weeks of unpaid leave available to parents of newborn or adopted children, to allow time for the bonding that is so essential to a child's social and emotional well-being.*

· *Flexible scheduling and job sharing should be available to employees to help them better balance work and family obligations.*

· *Parents of preschool children should be given at least two parenting days off each year, with pay, to visit with their children in day-care and preschool programs, and to consult with teachers.*

· *All employers should help their workers gain access to high-quality child-care and preschool services, either on-site or at local centers. A child-care information and referral service also should be available to workers.*

· *A national clearinghouse should be established, perhaps by the National Alliance of Business, to help employers promote family-friendly work policies.*

TELEVISION AS TEACHER

NEXT TO PARENTS, television is the child's most influential teacher. School readiness requires television programming that is both educational and enriching.

- *Each of the major commercial networks—CBS, NBC, ABC, and Fox—should offer, at an appropriate time, at least one hour of preschool educational programming every week.*

- *A Ready-to-Learn television guide should be prepared, listing programs on all channels that have special educational value for young children.*

- *Companies producing and selling products geared to young children—toys, breakfast cereals, fast foods—should help underwrite quality educational television for preschoolers.*

- *Every hour of children's programming on commercial networks should include at least one sixty-second Ready-to-Learn message that focuses on the physical, social, or educational needs of children.*

- *Twenty million dollars should now be appropriated to the National Endowment for Children's Educational Television to support the creation of educational programs for preschoolers.*

- *A Ready-to-Learn cable channel should be established, working collaboratively with public television, to offer program-*

ming aimed exclusively at the educational needs and interests of preschool children.

- *A National Conference on Children's Television should be convened to bring together broadcast executives, corporate sponsors, educators, and children's advocates to design a decade-long school-readiness television strategy.*

Step Six

Neighborhoods for Learning

Since all children need spaces and places for growth and exploration, safe and friendly neighborhoods are needed, ones that contribute richly to a child's readiness to learn.

- *A network of well-designed outdoor and indoor parks should be created in every community to give preschoolers opportunities for exercise and exploration.*

- *"Street playgrounds" should be established in every urban area to make open spaces for creative play and learning immediately available to children.*

- *Every library, museum, and zoo should establish a school-readiness program for preschoolers. The funding of such services should be given top priority by each community.*

- *Every major shopping mall should include in its facility a Ready-to-Learn Center, an inviting, creative space where young children can engage in play and learning.*

- *A Ready-to-Learn Youth Service Corps should be organized to make it possible for school and college students to serve as volunteers in children's Ready-to-Learn Centers, libraries, and playgrounds in every community.*

Step Seven

CONNECTIONS ACROSS THE GENERATIONS

CONNECTIONS across the generations will give children a sense of security and continuity, contributing to their school readiness in the fullest sense.

- *Schools, day-care centers, and retirement villages should redesign their programs to bring young and old together, building bridges across the generations.*

- *A ''Grandteacher Program'' should be created in communities across the country, one in which older people participate as mentors in day-care centers and preschools.*

- *Every community should organize a series of intergenerational projects—called ''Grand Days'' perhaps—in which senior citizens engage in activities and excursions with young children.*

Appendices

NATIONAL SURVEY OF KINDERGARTEN TEACHERS, 1991

Table 1

School Readiness: Percentage of Students Not Ready to Participate Successfully

ALL TEACHERS	35%
Alabama	36
Alaska	34
Arizona	35
Arkansas	42
California	38
Colorado	32
Connecticut	24
Delaware	42
Florida	38
Georgia	41
Hawaii	47
Idaho	26
Illinois	31
Indiana	32
Iowa	25
Kansas	27
Kentucky	40
Louisiana	39
Maine	30
Maryland	31
Massachusetts	26
Michigan	27
Minnesota	24
Mississippi	41
Missouri	33
Montana	28
Nebraska	29
Nevada	39
New Hampshire	29
New Jersey	27
New Mexico	40
New York	36
North Carolina	39
North Dakota	23
Ohio	33
Oklahoma	40
Oregon	32
Pennsylvania	29
Rhode Island	40
South Carolina	40
South Dakota	29
Tennessee	39
Texas	37
Utah	26
Vermont	28
Virginia	34
Washington	33
West Virginia	34
Wisconsin	32
Wyoming	26

SOURCE: The Carnegie Foundation for the Advancement of Teaching, National Survey of Kindergarten Teachers, 1991.

149

Table 2

Language Richness: How Serious a Problem Was Language Richness for Those Students
Who Entered School Not Ready to Learn?

	NO PROBLEM	SLIGHT PROBLEM	MODERATE PROBLEM	SERIOUS PROBLEM
ALL TEACHERS	2%	10%	37%	51%
Alabama	1	12	39	48
Alaska	2	17	27	54
Arizona	2	7	40	51
Arkansas	1	4	35	60
California	2	12	31	56
Colorado	2	13	35	50
Connecticut	0	11	46	43
Delaware	0	4	29	67
Florida	0	5	42	53
Georgia	1	4	31	64
Hawaii	0	4	37	59
Idaho	3	22	33	42
Illinois	3	10	39	48
Indiana	1	10	35	55
Iowa	2	15	48	35
Kansas	2	11	42	45
Kentucky	1	8	36	55
Louisiana	3	6	35	56
Maine	3	10	45	41
Maryland	1	8	43	48
Massachusetts	3	14	42	41
Michigan	3	12	42	43
Minnesota	1	13	52	33
Mississippi	1	8	33	59
Missouri	2	7	43	48
Montana	4	19	39	38
Nebraska	2	11	38	49
Nevada	1	10	45	45
New Hampshire	2	11	45	42
New Jersey	3	12	44	42
New Mexico	2	9	41	48
New York	1	12	40	47
North Carolina	2	10	31	57
North Dakota	6	22	43	28
Ohio	1	8	30	61
Oklahoma	1	16	38	45
Oregon	2	13	40	45
Pennsylvania	2	10	34	54
Rhode Island	0	11	23	66
South Carolina	0	7	27	66
South Dakota	2	11	40	48
Tennessee	1	11	34	54
Texas	1	13	35	50
Utah	1	18	50	32
Vermont	1	16	40	43
Virginia	2	7	35	56
Washington	0	13	38	49
West Virginia	1	12	27	60
Wisconsin	4	12	41	44
Wyoming	4	12	48	36

SOURCE: The Carnegie Foundation for the Advancement of Teaching, National Survey of Kindergarten Teachers, 1991.

150

Table 3

Emotional Maturity: How Serious a Problem Was Emotional Maturity for Those Students
Who Entered School Not Ready to Learn?

	NO PROBLEM	SLIGHT PROBLEM	MODERATE PROBLEM	SERIOUS PROBLEM
ALL TEACHERS	2%	12%	43%	43%
Alabama	2	10	47	41
Alaska	2	17	48	33
Arizona	1	19	41	39
Arkansas	2	15	51	32
California	2	11	43	45
Colorado	2	10	44	44
Connecticut	0	16	40	44
Delaware	0	8	53	39
Florida	1	10	41	48
Georgia	0	14	45	41
Hawaii	2	15	52	31
Idaho	3	17	45	36
Illinois	1	14	54	30
Indiana	1	12	45	41
Iowa	2	16	50	32
Kansas	0	11	47	42
Kentucky	2	14	45	39
Louisiana	2	12	43	43
Maine	1	12	42	45
Maryland	1	15	35	49
Massachusetts	1	7	43	49
Michigan	3	9	41	47
Minnesota	2	11	46	42
Mississippi	2	13	48	37
Missouri	0	15	47	38
Montana	2	14	44	39
Nebraska	2	17	44	38
Nevada	1	12	42	45
New Hampshire	2	11	35	52
New Jersey	4	11	44	41
New Mexico	3	13	47	37
New York	0	11	49	40
North Carolina	1	12	45	43
North Dakota	5	11	47	37
Ohio	1	6	46	47
Oklahoma	0	12	46	43
Oregon	1	11	41	48
Pennsylvania	0	13	35	51
Rhode Island	0	11	43	46
South Carolina	1	15	51	32
South Dakota	2	10	49	39
Tennessee	2	17	35	46
Texas	4	15	39	42
Utah	2	19	44	36
Vermont	1	14	48	37
Virginia	1	12	41	46
Washington	1	14	41	44
West Virginia	2	12	41	45
Wisconsin	4	17	37	42
Wyoming	3	21	36	40

SOURCE: The Carnegie Foundation for the Advancement of Teaching, National Survey of Kindergarten Teachers, 1991.

Table 4

General Knowledge: How Serious a Problem Was General Knowledge for Those
Students Who Entered School Not Ready to Learn?

	NO PROBLEM	SLIGHT PROBLEM	MODERATE PROBLEM	SERIOUS PROBLEM
ALL TEACHERS	2%	15%	45%	38%
Alabama	3	13	44	40
Alaska	2	23	40	35
Arizona	5	15	48	32
Arkansas	0	12	51	38
California	2	13	41	45
Colorado	4	16	45	36
Connecticut	3	17	46	34
Delaware	0	6	39	55
Florida	0	20	42	38
Georgia	0	12	41	47
Hawaii	1	10	50	39
Idaho	4	22	45	29
Illinois	2	15	44	39
Indiana	2	11	49	39
Iowa	4	17	54	24
Kansas	2	15	50	33
Kentucky	1	8	51	41
Louisiana	3	15	37	45
Maine	8	16	48	27
Maryland	2	14	46	39
Massachusetts	2	27	43	28
Michigan	5	22	45	28
Minnesota	1	25	46	28
Mississippi	2	9	49	40
Missouri	3	11	48	39
Montana	6	20	49	25
Nebraska	4	20	45	31
Nevada	3	14	39	44
New Hampshire	2	23	51	25
New Jersey	4	21	47	28
New Mexico	3	15	40	42
New York	2	18	47	32
North Carolina	1	13	48	37
North Dakota	5	23	50	23
Ohio	3	11	46	40
Oklahoma	1	15	50	34
Oregon	4	17	43	36
Pennsylvania	4	22	41	34
Rhode Island	0	23	34	43
South Carolina	1	7	46	46
South Dakota	2	20	47	31
Tennessee	1	14	41	44
Texas	3	13	46	39
Utah	1	18	49	32
Vermont	6	21	46	27
Virginia	1	14	43	42
Washington	1	18	54	27
West Virginia	0	17	43	40
Wisconsin	3	19	44	34
Wyoming	8	19	45	29

SOURCE: The Carnegie Foundation for the Advancement of Teaching, National Survey of Kindergarten Teachers, 1991.

152

Table 5
Social Confidence: How Serious a Problem Was Social Confidence for Those Students
Who Entered School Not Ready to Learn?

	NO PROBLEM	SLIGHT PROBLEM	MODERATE PROBLEM	SERIOUS PROBLEM
ALL TEACHERS	2%	19%	49%	31%
Alabama	3	19	46	31
Alaska	1	20	51	28
Arizona	1	14	48	37
Arkansas	1	20	55	24
California	3	19	47	31
Colorado	1	9	49	41
Connecticut	1	18	47	34
Delaware	0	13	62	25
Florida	1	20	45	34
Georgia	1	16	54	29
Hawaii	1	17	53	29
Idaho	4	21	53	22
Illinois	1	22	48	30
Indiana	1	22	47	30
Iowa	2	24	42	31
Kansas	1	20	49	30
Kentucky	1	15	49	36
Louisiana	2	18	41	40
Maine	1	20	53	27
Maryland	0	14	58	28
Massachusetts	0	14	59	27
Michigan	2	12	52	34
Minnesota	1	18	52	29
Mississippi	3	20	47	29
Missouri	2	21	53	25
Montana	4	24	49	24
Nebraska	2	17	44	36
Nevada	2	24	51	24
New Hampshire	0	15	52	33
New Jersey	3	25	46	26
New Mexico	4	21	51	24
New York	2	18	53	27
North Carolina	2	15	43	39
North Dakota	5	14	57	25
Ohio	3	13	54	30
Oklahoma	1	21	51	26
Oregon	0	15	51	34
Pennsylvania	2	16	50	31
Rhode Island	0	17	47	36
South Carolina	3	15	48	34
South Dakota	3	17	53	27
Tennessee	1	22	41	36
Texas	1	23	45	31
Utah	1	30	46	22
Vermont	3	18	51	28
Virginia	1	10	57	32
Washington	0	16	46	39
West Virginia	1	22	49	28
Wisconsin	2	18	47	32
Wyoming	2	26	48	24

SOURCE: The Carnegie Foundation for the Advancement of Teaching, National Survey of Kindergarten Teachers, 1991.

153

Table 6

Moral Awareness: How Serious a Problem Was Moral Awareness for Those Students
Who Entered School Not Ready to Learn?

	NO PROBLEM	SLIGHT PROBLEM	MODERATE PROBLEM	SERIOUS PROBLEM
ALL TEACHERS	10%	30%	39%	21%
Alabama	7	30	42	21
Alaska	16	29	39	16
Arizona	15	34	34	18
Arkansas	6	29	45	19
California	13	26	39	22
Colorado	9	24	42	25
Connecticut	20	31	34	14
Delaware	10	25	48	17
Florida	7	18	42	33
Georgia	5	27	44	24
Hawaii	8	34	48	10
Idaho	13	38	36	12
Illinois	13	40	31	16
Indiana	9	34	40	17
Iowa	11	37	34	18
Kansas	13	33	42	12
Kentucky	5	29	42	24
Louisiana	7	20	48	25
Maine	11	35	39	15
Maryland	8	33	37	22
Massachusetts	16	25	37	22
Michigan	13	30	42	15
Minnesota	10	36	41	14
Mississippi	9	22	35	35
Missouri	10	26	37	27
Montana	18	39	33	10
Nebraska	13	31	34	22
Nevada	15	22	43	21
New Hampshire	13	38	38	11
New Jersey	18	30	39	13
New Mexico	8	40	38	14
New York	10	34	38	17
North Carolina	6	24	37	33
North Dakota	19	35	31	15
Ohio	11	25	44	20
Oklahoma	7	38	34	20
Oregon	12	32	42	14
Pennsylvania	7	36	39	18
Rhode Island	13	33	39	15
South Carolina	5	35	34	26
South Dakota	13	37	35	14
Tennessee	10	24	42	24
Texas	7	31	38	24
Utah	12	35	38	16
Vermont	17	40	30	13
Virginia	11	30	41	18
Washington	11	32	45	13
West Virginia	15	38	33	14
Wisconsin	10	31	37	22
Wyoming	16	39	27	18

SOURCE: The Carnegie Foundation for the Advancement of Teaching, National Survey of Kindergarten Teachers, 1991.

154

Table 7

Physical Well-Being: How Serious a Problem Was Physical Well-Being for Those
Students Who Entered School Not Ready to Learn?

	NO PROBLEM	SLIGHT PROBLEM	MODERATE PROBLEM	SERIOUS PROBLEM
ALL TEACHERS	26%	40%	27%	6%
Alabama	32	40	25	3
Alaska	22	43	27	9
Arizona	23	37	31	9
Arkansas	15	44	36	5
California	18	42	31	9
Colorado	24	37	31	8
Connecticut	39	33	25	3
Delaware	13	60	23	4
Florida	21	38	34	7
Georgia	22	39	31	8
Hawaii	37	44	16	2
Idaho	17	51	25	7
Illinois	36	37	24	3
Indiana	29	37	30	4
Iowa	33	41	24	2
Kansas	27	42	26	5
Kentucky	20	40	31	10
Louisiana	31	33	32	4
Maine	28	36	28	8
Maryland	29	45	22	3
Massachusetts	39	35	24	3
Michigan	29	39	26	5
Minnesota	27	47	19	6
Mississippi	27	41	29	3
Missouri	18	51	26	5
Montana	31	39	25	6
Nebraska	32	37	22	9
Nevada	29	31	33	7
New Hampshire	24	45	26	5
New Jersey	44	34	19	3
New Mexico	21	42	28	9
New York	31	34	31	4
North Carolina	23	47	25	5
North Dakota	41	43	15	1
Ohio	28	41	24	7
Oklahoma	25	48	25	3
Oregon	20	30	39	11
Pennsylvania	34	41	23	2
Rhode Island	33	33	24	9
South Carolina	21	51	23	5
South Dakota	28	33	30	9
Tennessee	29	43	25	4
Texas	28	42	25	5
Utah	33	50	11	6
Vermont	28	33	30	9
Virginia	31	42	23	3
Washington	15	41	35	10
West Virginia	21	45	24	10
Wisconsin	24	43	29	4
Wyoming	39	28	24	9

SOURCE: The Carnegie Foundation for the Advancement of Teaching, National Survey of Kindergarten Teachers, 1991.

Table 8

Five-Year Change: How Does the Readiness of Your Students
Compare to Five Years Ago?

	FEWER READY TO LEARN	ABOUT THE SAME	MORE READY TO LEARN
ALL TEACHERS	43%	33%	25%
Alabama	38	28	35
Alaska	48	27	25
Arizona	42	34	25
Arkansas	44	29	27
California	53	32	15
Colorado	47	32	21
Connecticut	40	38	22
Delaware	35	53	12
Florida	52	22	26
Georgia	41	29	30
Hawaii	38	43	20
Idaho	34	38	29
Illinois	35	27	38
Indiana	35	35	30
Iowa	38	42	20
Kansas	40	36	24
Kentucky	35	27	38
Louisiana	32	27	41
Maine	49	36	15
Maryland	40	38	22
Massachusetts	35	44	21
Michigan	39	39	22
Minnesota	41	34	25
Mississippi	34	36	30
Missouri	39	28	33
Montana	34	43	23
Nebraska	49	38	13
Nevada	48	28	24
New Hampshire	37	30	33
New Jersey	38	35	28
New Mexico	37	39	25
New York	46	35	19
North Carolina	49	32	19
North Dakota	27	37	36
Ohio	46	32	22
Oklahoma	54	30	17
Oregon	47	35	18
Pennsylvania	35	36	29
Rhode Island	55	21	24
South Carolina	49	26	25
South Dakota	41	37	23
Tennessee	46	30	25
Texas	37	35	27
Utah	30	36	34
Vermont	30	39	31
Virginia	29	33	38
Washington	44	40	16
West Virginia	35	36	29
Wisconsin	56	27	18
Wyoming	34	37	28

SOURCE: The Carnegie Foundation for the Advancement of Teaching, National Survey of Kindergarten Teachers, 1991.

156

Table 9

Which One of the Following Goals Is the Most Important?

	IMPROVE PARENT EDUCATION	MORE FUNDING FOR PRE-SCHOOLS	DECREASE TV VIEWING	BETTER HEALTH SERVICES	MORE WORKPLACE POLICIES	SAFER NEIGHBOR-HOODS	OTHER
ALL TEACHERS	64%	16%	5%	1%	5%	2%	7%
Alabama	76	13	1	1	4	1	4
Alaska	59	11	9	0	8	0	13
Arizona	57	19	3	3	7	1	11
Arkansas	68	18	3	0	5	1	5
California	56	21	4	2	2	2	13
Colorado	66	10	5	2	8	2	8
Connecticut	61	14	10	0	6	3	7
Delaware	75	10	2	0	6	2	6
Florida	67	16	4	1	5	3	5
Georgia	66	20	0	1	7	1	3
Hawaii	66	24	2	0	4	1	3
Idaho	65	12	8	1	8	1	6
Illinois	67	13	7	1	5	2	4
Indiana	58	17	6	2	10	0	7
Iowa	62	17	10	1	4	1	5
Kansas	64	15	7	1	3	1	8
Kentucky	67	19	3	0	5	0	6
Louisiana	53	24	2	0	7	2	12
Maine	64	14	7	2	5	0	9
Maryland	58	16	7	1	5	1	12
Massachusetts	49	20	7	2	5	5	13
Michigan	72	12	4	1	4	1	6
Minnesota	58	16	10	1	9	0	7
Mississippi	78	13	3	0	3	1	3
Missouri	66	8	8	1	8	1	8
Montana	73	9	6	0	6	0	6
Nebraska	63	14	6	0	9	0	6
Nevada	64	10	10	2	6	0	8
New Hampshire	65	13	3	2	7	2	8
New Jersey	64	15	7	2	4	2	7
New Mexico	61	18	1	1	6	1	11
New York	62	15	5	3	8	1	6
North Carolina	64	18	3	1	5	1	8
North Dakota	57	13	9	0	10	0	11
Ohio	62	15	4	1	7	1	10
Oklahoma	67	10	8	3	4	1	7
Oregon	54	13	7	2	7	1	15
Pennsylvania	64	16	4	0	7	3	7
Rhode Island	61	5	14	2	7	2	9
South Carolina	67	23	2	0	4	0	4
South Dakota	63	16	8	1	6	1	6
Tennessee	66	13	4	1	4	1	11
Texas	72	13	5	0	5	3	3
Utah	65	9	10	3	3	2	8
Vermont	68	14	6	3	6	2	2
Virginia	61	21	3	1	7	1	5
Washington	62	17	6	3	4	2	6
West Virginia	66	19	3	1	4	1	7
Wisconsin	66	13	4	0	6	4	8
Wyoming	70	15	3	0	5	0	7

SOURCE: The Carnegie Foundation for the Advancement of Teaching, National Survey of Kindergarten Teachers, 1991.

Table 10
Class Size: Full-Day Kindergarten

ALL TEACHERS	23
Alabama	20
Alaska	25
Arizona	24
Arkansas	20
California	27
Colorado	25
Connecticut	21
Delaware	11
Florida	25
Georgia	22
Hawaii	24
Idaho	26
Illinois	25
Indiana	25
Iowa	24
Kansas	24
Kentucky	21
Louisiana	23
Maine	18
Maryland	24
Massachusetts	23
Michigan	30
Minnesota	25
Mississippi	25
Missouri	23
Montana	17
Nebraska	22
Nevada	31
New Hampshire	16
New Jersey	22
New Mexico	21
New York	24
North Carolina	26
North Dakota	19
Ohio	26
Oklahoma	22
Oregon	30
Pennsylvania	24
Rhode Island	22
South Carolina	27
South Dakota	21
Tennessee	24
Texas	20
Utah	47
Vermont	13
Virginia	23
Washington	26
West Virginia	23
Wisconsin	24
Wyoming	17

SOURCE: The Carnegie Foundation for the Advancement of Teaching, National Survey of Kindergarten Teachers, 1991.

158

Table 11

Class Size: A.M. Kindergarten

ALL TEACHERS	23
Alabama	20
Alaska	23
Arizona	23
Arkansas	20
California	29
Colorado	24
Connecticut	20
Delaware	21
Florida	22
Georgia	12
Hawaii	NA
Idaho	22
Illinois	23
Indiana	21
Iowa	23
Kansas	20
Kentucky	23
Louisiana	18
Maine	17
Maryland	23
Massachusetts	21
Michigan	23
Minnesota	24
Mississippi	24
Missouri	23
Montana	19
Nebraska	22
Nevada	26
New Hampshire	19
New Jersey	21
New Mexico	18
New York	21
North Carolina	NA
North Dakota	21
Ohio	24
Oklahoma	20
Oregon	22
Pennsylvania	23
Rhode Island	22
South Carolina	25
South Dakota	21
Tennessee	21
Texas	21
Utah	27
Vermont	16
Virginia	21
Washington	23
West Virginia	18
Wisconsin	22
Wyoming	21

NA = Not Applicable

SOURCE: The Carnegie Foundation for the Advancement of Teaching, National Survey of Kindergarten Teachers, 1991.

159

Table 12
Class Size: P.M. Kindergarten

ALL TEACHERS	23
Alabama	NA
Alaska	23
Arizona	22
Arkansas	19
California	30
Colorado	23
Connecticut	19
Delaware	20
Florida	23
Georgia	10
Hawaii	22
Idaho	21
Illinois	23
Indiana	20
Iowa	22
Kansas	20
Kentucky	22
Louisiana	NA
Maine	18
Maryland	22
Massachusetts	21
Michigan	23
Minnesota	23
Mississippi	24
Missouri	23
Montana	20
Nebraska	21
Nevada	25
New Hampshire	18
New Jersey	20
New Mexico	18
New York	21
North Carolina	27
North Dakota	23
Ohio	24
Oklahoma	20
Oregon	22
Pennsylvania	22
Rhode Island	21
South Carolina	24
South Dakota	22
Tennessee	NA
Texas	21
Utah	26
Vermont	16
Virginia	21
Washington	22
West Virginia	18
Wisconsin	22
Wyoming	20

NA = Not Applicable

SOURCE: The Carnegie Foundation for the Advancement of Teaching, National Survey of Kindergarten Teachers, 1991.

Appendix B

Technical Notes

THE CARNEGIE FOUNDATION for the Advancement of Teaching's *National Survey of Kindergarten Teachers, 1991,* was administered by The Wirthlin Group of McLean, Virginia. The purpose of this research effort was to record the opinions of kindergarten teachers regarding the readiness of children who entered their classes in the fall of 1990. In August 1991, questionnaires were mailed to 20,684 kindergarten teachers in all fifty states. Responses were received from 7,141 teachers, which represents a completion rate of 34.5 percent.

A stratified random sample design was used for this survey. Teachers' names were drawn from alphabetized lists of public school kindergarten teachers employed in each state. Market Data Retrieval of Shelton, Connecticut, maintains the lists, which include the names of approximately 75 percent of all public school teachers in the United States.

Using a fixed sample size from each state does not allow for differences between states in terms of the total population of kindergarten teachers. A weighting scheme was developed so that the survey response would represent the relative numbers of teachers in the fifty states.

The results of any sample survey are subject to sampling variations. The magnitude of the variations is measurable, and it is affected by a number of factors, including the number of completed questionnaires and the level of percentages expressing the results.

A national survey of public school teachers was conducted in both 1987 and 1990. In each study questionnaires were mailed to 40,000 elementary and secondary teachers. The details of these surveys are reported in the technical reports *The Condition of Teaching: A State-by-State Analysis, 1988* and *The Condition of Teaching: A State-by-State Analysis, 1990.*

161

The *Survey of Fifth- and Eighth-Graders* was administered in the Fall of 1988 by The Carnegie Foundation. Questionnaires were completed by 2,750 fifth-grade students and 2,906 eighth-grade students. They were asked to respond to questions about their preferences for school subjects, coping with personal problems, feelings about the environments in which they live, and participation in activities beyond the classroom.

The Carnegie Foundation conducted the *Survey of Kindergarten Parents* in the Fall of 1987. Almost 2,000 parents answered questions about the preschool experience, the kindergarten curriculum, the habits of young children, and policies related to the care of young children.

For additional information on the data presented in this report, contact The Carnegie Foundation for the Advancement of Teaching, Data and Trends Analysis, 5 Ivy Lane, Princeton, NJ 08540.

162

America's First Goal: Readiness for All

1. The Carnegie Foundation for the Advancement of Teaching, National Survey of Kindergarten Teachers, 1991. All quotations from kindergarten teachers are taken from this survey.

2. Ashley Montagu, *Growing Young,* 2d ed. (New York: Bergin & Garvey, 1989), 121.

3. Harold Hodgkinson, "Reform Versus Reality," *Phi Delta Kappan* (September 1991): 10.

4. Southern Regional Education Board, "Goals for Education: Challenge 2000" (Atlanta, GA: 1988), 5.

5. Carnegie, National Survey of Kindergarten Teachers, 1991.

6. Kenneth Keniston and the Carnegie Council on Children, *All Our Children: The American Family Under Pressure* (New York: Carnegie Corporation of New York, 1977), 18.

7. Walter Lippmann, *An Inquiry into the Principles of the Good Society* (Boston: Little, Brown and Company, 1937), 348.

8. Tom Bradbury, "Editorial Notebook: A Strong Team for Children," *The Charlotte Observer,* 14 August 1991, 16A.

9. Sylvia Ann Hewlett, *When the Bough Breaks: The Cost of Neglecting Our Children* (New York: Basic Books, 1991), 282–83.

The First Step: A Healthy Start

1. James Agee and Walker Evans, *Three Tenant Families: Let Us Now Praise Famous Men* (Boston: Houghton Mifflin Company, 1941).

163

2. U.S. Bureau of the Census, Department of Commerce; figures are for 1990. Also, personal communication, Martin O'Connell, with the census bureau, December 1991.

3. "Essential Components of a Successful Education System," *The Business Roundtable Education Public Policy Agenda*, 1991, 2.

4. *Historical Statistics of the United States: Colonial Times to 1970*, Part I, U.S. Department of Commerce, 1975, 60; and *U.S. Children and Their Families: Current Conditions and Recent Trends, 1989* (Washington: U.S. Government Printing Office, 1989), A7, 1310–17.

5. Physician Task Force on Hunger in America, *Hunger in America: The Growing Epidemic* (Middletown, CT: Wesleyan University Press, 1985), 8–9, 17; and Food Research and Action Center, Community Childhood Hunger Identification Project (Washington, DC: 1991) v.

6. Lucile Newman and Stephen L. Buka, *Every Child a Learner: Reducing Risks of Learning Impairment During Pregnancy and Infancy* (Denver: Education Commission of the States, 1990), 17–18.

7. Scott R. Creel and Jack L. Albright, "Early Experience," *Veterinary Clinics of North America—Food Animal Practice*, 1987, vol. 3, no. 2, 251–68.

8. Newman and Buka, *Every Child a Learner*, 8.

9. Irving B. Harris, "Education—Does It Make Any Difference When You Start?", speech to the Forum of the City Club of Cleveland, 15 December 1989.

10. Newman and Buka, *Every Child a Learner*, 5.

11. Newman and Buka, *Every Child a Learner*, 5–6.

12. B. S. Worthington-Roberts et al., *Nutrition in Pregnancy and Lactation* (St. Louis: Mosby Yearbook, Inc., 1985), 1.

13. Newman and Buka, *Every Child a Learner*, 8–10.

14. Lloyd D. Johnston et al., *Trends in Drug Use and Associated Factors Among American High School Students, College Students, and Young Adults: 1975–1989* (National Institute on Drug Abuse, 1991), table 10.

164

15. Kenneth H. Cooper, *Kid Fitness: A Complete Shape-Up Program from Birth Through High School* (New York: Bantam Books, 1991), 1–2.

16. The Carnegie Foundation for the Advancement of Teaching, *The Condition of Teaching: A State-by-State Analysis*, 1988 and 1990 (Princeton, NJ: Carnegie Foundation, 1988 and 1990).

17. Ramon C. Cortines, ''A Practitioner's Perspective on the Interrelationship of the Health and Education of Children'' (Washington, DC: National Health/Education Consortium, May 1991), 3.

18. Robert H. Bremner, ed., *Children and Youth in America: A Documentary History, Volume II: 1866–1932*, Parts Seven and Eight (Cambridge, MA: Harvard University Press, 1971), 1059–62.

19. Personal communication, Fran Kaufman, The New York Academy of Medicine, November 1991.

20. Libby Blank, Presentation to District 8 Principals Meeting, Anne Frank School, 15 March 1991.

21. American Health Education publications, 1991.

22. Phyllis L. Ellickson and Robert M. Bell, ''Drug Prevention in Junior High: A Multi-Site Longitudinal Test,'' *Science,* vol. 247, 16 March 1990, 1299–1304.

23. ''Interrelationship of the Health and Education of Children,'' National Health/Education Consortium, May 1991, 5.

24. Metropolitan Life Foundation, Humphrey Taylor et al., Louis Harris and Associates, *Health You've Got to be Taught: An Evaluation of Comprehensive Health Education in American Public Schools* (New York: January-May 1988), 5.

25. ''Interrelationship of the Health and Education of Children,'' National Health/Education Consortium, May 1991, 6.

26. Betty Watts Carrington, Columbia University, ''The Effects of Socioeconomic Factors, Especially Poverty, Malnutrition, Environment and the Medicalization of Pregnancy and Childbirth on Learning Outcomes,'' paper prepared for Carnegie, June 1988).

27. Food Research and Action Center, December 1991 figures; personal communication, Geraldine Henchy.

28. "National Evaluation of the Special Supplement Food Program for Women, Infants, and Children (WIC)," *The American Journal of Clinical Nutrition,* vol. 48, no. 2 (August 1988).

29. "Estimated Funding for WIC Applicants," Food Research and Action Center, March 13, 1991; United States Department of Agriculture study, October 1991, estimates that for every dollar spent on a pregnant woman in the WIC program, the savings in Medicaid costs to the mother and newborn is now $4.21.

30. "Estimated Funding for WIC Applicants," Food Research and Action Center, 13 March 1991.

31. *The Oxford Dictionary of Quotations*, 3rd ed. (Oxford, England: Oxford University Press, 1980), 150.

32. *Healthy Brain Development: Precursor to Learning,* Natural Health/Education Consortium, 1991, 2.

33. Newman and Buka, *Every Child a Learner*.

34. Susheela Singh, Jacqueline Darroch Forrest, and Aida Torres, "Prenatal Care in the United States: A State and County Inventory" (New York: The Alan Guttmacher Institute, 1989), v–vi.

35. Ibid.

36. Lisbeth B. Schorr with Daniel Schorr, *Within Our Reach: Breaking the Cycle of Disadvantage* (New York: Anchor Press, 1988), 68.

37. Children's Defense Fund figures; see also *S.O.S. America! A Children's Defense Budget* (Washington, DC, 1990), 14, 71–4.

38. National Center for Children in Poverty, *Five Million Children: A Statistical Profile of Our Poorest Young Citizens* (New York, 1990), 64.

39. *A Healthy America: The Challenge for States,* The National Governors' Association (Washington, DC: 1991), 25.

40. William M. McClatchey, "The Forgotten Crisis in Rural Health Care," *The Atlanta Journal/The Atlanta Constitution,* 15 September 1991, Section G1.

41. *A Healthy America: The Challenge for States,* The National Governors' Association (Washington, DC: 1991), 26.

42. *A Healthy America,* 9.

43. Children's Defense Fund, *S.O.S. America! A Children's Defense Budget* (Washington, DC: 1990), 7.

44. "Making Connections: Adolescents," The Robert Wood Johnson Foundation, Princeton, NJ, 1991, 1.

45. Lynn R. Goldman, American Academy of Pediatrics testimony to the U.S. Senate Environment and Public Works Committee, 27 June 1990.

46. "From the Surgeon General, U.S. Public Health Service," *Journal of the American Medical Association*, vol. 265, no. 11, 20 March 1991, 1364.

47. California State Department of Education, news release, December 7, 1988.

48. National Commission on Children, *Beyond Rhetoric: A New American Agenda for Children and Families* (Washington, DC: U.S. Government Printing Office, 1991), 46.

49. Personal communication, Aaron Shirley, MD, November 1991.

50. "Interrelationship of the Health and Education of Children."

The Second Step: Empowered Parents

1. Mary E. Clark, "Meaningful Social Bonding as a Universal Human Need," in *Conflict: Human Needs Theory*, John W. Burton, ed. (New York: St. Martin's Press, 1990), 34.

2. Daniel Goleman, "The Experience of Touch: Research Points to a Critical Role," *The New York Times*, 2 February 1988, C1.

3. National Commission on Children, 46.

4. Diane Ackerman, *A Natural History of the Senses* (New York: Vintage Books, 1990), 178–79.

5. Lewis Thomas, *Late Night Thoughts on Listening to Mahler's Ninth Symphony* (New York: Viking Press, 1983), 52.

6. Genevieve Clapp, *Child Study Research: Current Perspectives and Applications* (Lexington, MA: Lexington Books, 1988), 192.

7. Hannah Nuba-Scheffler et al., *Infancy: A Guide to Research and Resources* (Teachers College Press, 1986), 143–54.

8. See also William R. Mattox, Jr., "The Parent Trap," *Policy Review*, Winter 1991, 6.

9. National Center for Education Statistics, 1991, in *The National Education Goals Report, 1991* (Washington, DC: The National Education Goals Panel, 1991), 36.

10. Howard Gardner, *Frames of Mind: The Theory of Multiple Intelligences* (New York: Basic Books, 1983).

11. *National Education Goals Report*, 36.

12. Louis Harris and Associates, 1986 and 1989.

13. Robert N. Bellah et al., *The Good Society* (New York: Alfred A. Knopf, 1991), 93.

14. Paul Taylor, "Surveys Find Americans Value Family Ties in Hard Times," *The Washington Post*, 21 November 1991, A3.

15. T. Berry Brazelton, "The Family Leave Act, From the Baby's Point of View," *The Wall Street Journal*, 19 September 1991, A15.

16. CBS Sunday Morning, 1988.

17. David Ayres and James L. Morris, "Bond and Bartman Announce Study Confirms Missouri Families and Children Gain from Parents as

Teachers Program,'' Office of Senator Christopher S. ''Kit'' Bond, Washington, DC, 2 July 1991.

18. ''HIPPY: The Home Instruction Program for Preschool Youngsters,'' National Council of Jewish Women (New York, 1990) 1–2.

19. Personal communication, David Leonard, November 1991.

20. Michel Marriott, ''When Parents and Children Go to School Together,'' *The New York Times*, 21 August 1991, B7.

21. *A Place to Start: The Kenan Trust Family Literacy Project* (Louisville, KY: The National Center for Family Literacy, 1989), 17.

22. Will Durant, *The Age of Faith* (New York: Simon and Schuster, 1950), 819.

The Third Step: Quality Preschool

1. Children's Defense Fund, *The State of America's Children, 1991* (Washington, DC: 1991), 37–39.

2. ''Essential Components of a Successful Education System,'' The Business Roundtable Education Public Policy Agenda, 6.

3. Interviews during site visit to child-care center, 1988.

4. Barbara Willer et al., *The Demand and Supply of Child Care in 1990* (Washington, DC: National Association for the Education of Young Children 1991), 43–45.

5. William Damon, *The Moral Child: Nurturing Children's Natural Moral Growth* (New York: The Free Press, 1988), 85–87.

6. Tiffany Field, ''Quality Infant Day-Care and Grade-School Behavior and Performance,'' *Child Development*, vol. 62, no. 4, August 1991, 863.

7. J. R. Lally et al., ''The Syracuse University Family Development Research Program: Long-Range Impact of an Early-Intervention with Low-Income Children and Their Families,'' in D. R. Powell, ed., *Par-

ent Education as Early Childhood Intervention: Emerging Directions in Theory, Research, and Practice (Norwood, NJ: Abler, 1988), 1.

8. Carl F. Kaestle, *Pillars of the Republic: Common Schools and American Society, 1780–1860* (New York: Hill and Wang, 1983), 31–32.

9. Margaret O'Brien Steinfels, *Who's Minding the Children? The History and Politics of Day Care in America* (New York: Simon and Schuster, 1973), 43. This source provided the historical discussion that follows.

10. Edward F. Zigler and Mary E. Lang, *Child Care Choices: Balancing the Needs of Children, Families, and Society* (New York: The Free Press, 1991), 41.

11. National Center for Education Statistics, 1991, in *The National Education Goals Report: Building a Nation of Learners* (Washington, DC: The National Education Goals Panel, 1991), 37.

12. Bret C. Williams and C. Arden Miller, *Preventive Health Care for Young Children: Findings from a 10-Country Study and Directions for United States Policy* (National Center for Clinical Infant Programs, 1991), 37.

13. Sheila B. Kamerman, "Child Care Policies and Programs: An International Overview," *Journal of Social Issues,* vol. 47, no. 2, 1991, 179.

14. Williams and Miller, *Preventive Health Care for Young Children.*

15. Sheila B. Kamerman, "An International Overview of Preschool Programs," *Phi Delta Kappan,* October 1989, 135–37.

16. Pia Hinkle, " 'A School Must Rest on the Idea that All Children Are Different,' " *Newsweek,* 2 December 1991, 53–54.

17. Personal communication, Inga Kraus, The Children's Center, SUNY, New Paltz, November 1991.

18. Leslie Baldacci, "Father of Head Start Visits His 'Kids,' " *Chicago Sun-Times,* 20 October 1991, 24.

19. Personal communication, Jan Carey, November 1991.

20. Valerie Lee et al., *Are Head Start Effects Sustained? A Longitudinal Follow-up Comparison of Disadvantaged Children Attending Head Start, No Preschool, and Other Preschool Programs,* U.S. Department of Education, ERIC ED, 309, 880, May 1989.

21. "Project Education Reform: Time for Results," Orangeburg School District Five; and personal communication, Myrtle McDaniels, November 1991.

22. R. Hubbell McKey et al., *The Impact of Head Start on Children, Families, and Communities: Final Report of the Head Start Evaluation, Synthesis and Utilization Project* (Washington, DC: U.S. Department of Health and Human Services, Administration for Children, Youth and Families, Head Start Bureau, 1985), 15–17, III–62–64.

23. David P. Weikart, *Quality Preschool Programs: A Long-Term Source Investment,* Occasional Paper Number Five, Ford Foundation Project on Social Welfare and the American Future (New York: Ford Foundation, 1989).

24. *The School Readiness Act, 1991, S.9-1-1* (Washington, DC: May 1991).

25. Committee for Economic Development, A Statement by the Research and Policy Committee, *The Unfinished Agenda: A New Vision for Child Development and Education* (Washington, DC: 1991), 11.

26. Anne Stewart et al., Congressional Research Service, "Head Start: Percentage of Eligible Children Served and Recent Expansions," *CRS Report for Congress* (Washington, DC: 30 July 1991), 1–6. *The School Readiness Act of 1991, S.9-1-1* (Washington, DC: May 1991).

27. Ibid.

28. Edward F. Zigler and Matia Finn Stevenson, "Child Care in America: From Problem to Solution," *Educational Policy 3,* no. 4, 1989, 322.

29. "Schools That Never Close," *Newsweek,* 15 May 1989, 60.

30. The Carnegie Foundation Survey Among Parents of Kindergarten Students, 1987.

31. Carol Lawson, "In Missouri, The 12-Hour Playday," *The New York Times*, 4 October 1990, C1.

32. Robert A. Frahm, "City School Program Addresses Community Needs," *The Hartford Courant*, 12 October 1990, A14.

33. The National Academy of Sciences study, 1991.

34. Personal communication, Boice Fowler, Department of Family Services, November 1991.

35. Gina C. Adams, *Who Knows How Safe? The Status of State Efforts to Ensure Quality Child Care* (Washington, DC: Children's Defense Fund, 1990); and *The State of America's Children*, 1991, 39.

36. Carnegie Foundation compilation, telephone survey, August 1991.

37. Paul Taylor, "Day Care: Soaring Popularity, Stable Cost," *The Washington Post*, 7 November 1991, A20.

38. Ellen Eliason Kisker et al., *A Profile of Child Care Settings* (Washington, DC: Mathematica Policy Research, Inc.), 1991.

39. Peter G. Peterson, "The Morning After," *The Atlantic Monthly*, October 1987; 63–64.

40. Fred M. Hechinger, "About Education," *The New York Times*, 1 August 1990, B8.

41. Kisker, *A Profile of Child-Care Settings*.

42. National Center for Education Statistics, personal communication, Vance Grant, November 1991. Figure reflects 1989 survey, the latest available.

The Fourth Step: A Responsive Workplace

1. "Today's Parents: How Well Are They Doing? A Report from the Editors of *Better Homes and Gardens*" (September 1986), 54.

2. Tamara Hareven, "Historical Changes in the Family and the Life

Course: Implications for Child Development''; in Alice B. Smuts and John W. Hagen, eds., *History and Research in Child Development,* monographs of the Society for Research in Child Development, vol. 50, no. 211 (1986) 17–19.

3.   Kenneth Keniston and the Carnegie Council on Children, *All Our Children: The American Family Under Pressure* (New York: Harcourt Brace Jovanovich, 1977), 14.

4.   Arlie Hochschild, *Second Shift: Working Parents and the Revolution at Home* (New York: Viking, 1989), 231, 267; in Robert N. Bellah et al., *The Good Society* (New York: Alfred A. Knopf, 1991), 48.

5.   ''What's Happening to American Families? A Report on American Families from the Editors of *Better Homes and Gardens*'' (October 1988), 93.

6.   Paul Taylor, ''Surveys Show Americans Turn to Family Ties in Hard Times,'' *The Washington Post*, 21 November 1991, A3.

7.   ''Today's Parents: How Well Are They Doing? A Report from the Editors of *Better Homes and Gardens*'' (September 1986), 6.

8.   Burton L. White, *The First Three Years of Life* (New York: Prentice Hall, 1990), 304.

9.   Kathleen Makuen, ''Public Servants, Private Parents: Parental Leave in the Public Sector''; in Edward F. Zigler and Meryl Frank, eds., *The Parental Leave Crisis: Toward a National Policy* (New Haven: Yale University Press, 1988), 196–97.

10.   Employee Benefit Research Institute, ''Public Attitudes on Child Care and Parental Leave'' (Washington, DC: Employee Benefit Research Institute, 1990); in *Report on Preschool Programs,* 13 March 1991, 57.

11.   Martin O'Connell and David E. Bloom, *Juggling Jobs and Babies: America's Child Care Challenge,* Population Trends and Public Policy, no. 12 (Washington, DC: Population Reference Bureau, 1987), 11.

12.   Edward F. Zigler and Meryl Frank, eds., *The Parental Leave Crisis: Toward a National Policy* (New Haven: Yale University Press, 1988), xxiii.

13. Joseph P. Allen, "European Infant Care Leaves: Foreign Perspectives on the Integration of Work and Family Leave Roles"; in Zigler and Frank, eds., *Parental Leave Crisis,* 247–53.

14. Eileen Trzcinski, "Leave Policies in Small Businesses: Findings from the U.S. Small Business Administration Employee Leave Survey"; in *Report on Preschool Programs,* 8 May 1991, 95.

15. Bellah et al., *The Good Society,* 260–61.

16. Personal communication, Cindy Maleychik, personnel, Joy Cone, November 1991.

17. Hal Morgan and Kerry Tucker, *Companies That Care* (New York: Simon and Schuster, 1991), 330–31.

18. Ibid., 183.

19. Ibid., 176; personal communication, Chris Gilmore, SAS Institute, November 1991.

20. Ibid., 174.

21. Personal communication, Joyce Rotgh, US West, November 1991.

22. Morgan and Tucker, *Companies That Care,* 315–16.

23. Ellen Galinsky, Testimony for the United States Senate Subcommittee on Children, Family, Drugs, and Alcoholism; Hearing on Balancing Work and Family: The Family and Medical Leave Act, 24 January 1991.

24. Ibid.

25. Survey Among Parents of Kindergarten Students, The Carnegie Foundation for the Advancement of Teaching, October 1987.

26. Bureau of National Affairs, "Employers and Child Care: Development of a New Employee Benefit"; in John P. Fernandez, *Child Care and Corporate Productivity: Resolving Family/Work Conflicts* (Lexington, MA: Lexington Books, 1986), 144.

27. Dana Priest, "Employees Caring for Children, Elders Need More Work Options, Study Says," *The Washington Post,* 13 November 1991, A17.

28. Personal communication, Terrence Marable, Pitney Bowes, November 1991.

29. Personal communication, Terry Loftus, Proctor & Gamble, September 1991.

30. Susan B. Dynerman and Lynn O. Hayes, *The Best Jobs in America for Parents Who Want Careers and Time for Children Too* (New York: Rawson Associates, 1991), 27.

31. David Blankenhorn, Steven Bayme, and Jean Bethke Elshtain, eds., *Rebuilding the Nest: A New Commitment to the American Family* (Milwaukee, WI: Family Service America, 1990), 213–15; personal communication, Dianna Lee, Human Resources, American Express, November 1991.

32. Personal communication, John Gregg, Office of the Governor, Boston, Massachusetts, on the remarks as delivered by Governor William F. Weld before the Committee on Educational Policy, Worcester, Massachusetts, 24 October 1991.

33. Personal communication, Terry Loftus, Proctor & Gamble, September 1991.

34. Morgan and Tucker, *Companies That Care,* 170; personal communication, Sandra Conway, NCNB, November 1991.

35. Personal communication, Charles Waters, *Hemmings Motor News,* Bennington, Vermont, November 1991.

36. Dana Friedman, "Corporate Financial Assistance for Child Care," *The Conference Board Research Bulletin,* vol. 177 (New York: The Conference Board, 1985), 4.

37. Morgan and Tucker, *Companies That Care,* 25.

38. Employee Benefit Research Institute, "Public Attitudes," 57.

39. Anne Summers, "15 Best Cities for Child Care," *Working Mother* (February 1991), 68.

40. Ann Gilman Dawson, Cynthia Sirk Mikel, Cheryl S. Lorenz, and Joel King, "An Experimental Study of the Effects of Employer-Sponsored Child Care Services on Selected Employee Behaviors"; in *Child Care: Employer Assistance for Private Sector and Federal Employees* (Washington, DC: General Accounting Office, 1986), 27–8.

41. Adam Seitchik, Jeffrey Zornitsky, Christopher Edmonds, *Employer Strategies for a Changing Labor Force: A Primer on Innovative Programs and Policies Research Report 90-01* (Washington, DC: National Commission for Employment Policy, 1990), 77.

42. Ibid.

43. Morgan and Tucker, *Companies That Care,* 156; personal communication, Amy Hess, Patagonia, November 1991.

44. Personal communication, Harriet Lipkin, attorney, Akin, Gump, Hauer, and Feld, Washington, DC, September 1991.

45. Personal communication, Beth Wallace, Ben and Jerry's, Waterbury, Vermont, September 1991.

46. Personal communication, John Boudreaux, International Business Machines, Purchase, New York, September 1991.

47. "Child Care Database Helps Employees Locate Options," *Report on Preschool Programs,* 24 October 1990, 214.

48. "Large Companies Take the Lead in Launching Child Care Programs," *Report on Preschool Programs*, 8 May 1991, 95-6.

49. Stephen E. Ewing, "Nourish Thy Children: Investing in Child Care to Nourish Corporate Productivity," *Vital Speeches of the Day*, vol. LVI, no. 17 (15 June 1990), 517–19.

The Fifth Step: Television as Teacher

1. E. B. White, "One Man's Meat," *Harper's Magazine,* vol. 177 (October 1938), 553.

2. If nineteen million preschoolers watch roughly two hours a day times 365 days a year, they watch 14 billion hours of TV a year; Robert M. Liebert and Joyce N. Sprafkin, *The Early Window* 3d ed. (Elmsford, New York: Pergamon Press, 1988), 5.

3. Genevieve Clapp, *Child Study Research* (Lexington, MA: Lexington Books, 1988), 71–72.

4. Bianca Bradbury, "Is Television Mama's Friend or Foe?" *Good Housekeeping,* November 1950, 58, 263.

5. Personal communication, Edward Palmer; see also *Television and America's Children: A Crisis of Neglect* (New York: Oxford University Press, 1988).

6. "Content Analysis of Children's Television Advertisements," Washington, DC, May 1991. The Center for Science in the Public Interest Reports that over two hundred commercials for high-sugar and high-fat junk food appear each Saturday morning.

7. Diane Radecki, "Cartoon Report," The National Coalition on Television Violence, Champaign, IL, April 1991.

8. Newton N. Minow, "How Vast the Wasteland Now?" (New York: Gannett Foundation Media Center, 1991), 13. Speech, Columbia University, New York, 9 May 1991.

9. Daniel R. Anderson testified before the U.S. Senate in the April 12, 1989 hearings on "Education, Competitiveness, and Children's Television"; see also "The Impact of Children's Education: Television's Influence on Cognitive Development," U.S. Department of Education, April 1988.

10. Inga Sonesson, *Forskolebarn och Television* [Elementary Schoolchildren and TV] (Stockholm: Esselte Studium, 1979), 206–208.

11. Howard Taras et al., "Children's Television-Viewing Habits and the Family Environment," *American Journal of Diseases of Children*, vol. 144, no. 3 (March 1990): 357–59.

12. Personal communication, Peggy Charren, president, Action for Children's Television, December 1991.

13. "ABC Learning Alliance: Back-To-School Planner (New York: ABC Community Relations, CIStems, Inc., 1991).

14. Liebert and Sprafkin, *The Early Window,* 41.

15. Ibid., 219.

16. Ibid., 232.

17. "Extending 'The Neighborhood' to Child Care," Public Broadcasting Foundation of Northwest Ohio, Toledo, 1991.

18. *CPB Report,* 18 November 1991, vol. 10, no. 23 (Washington, DC: Corporation for Public Broadcasting).

19. John Wilner, "Preschool Series to Teach Life Skills," *Current: The Public Telecommunications Newspaper,* vols. 1 and 7, 18 November 1991.

20. Liebert and Sprafkin, *The Early Window,* 166.

21. Ibid., 12.

22. Peggy Charren, *ACT: The First 20 Years,* 1988, Action for Children's Television, 1.

23. Personal communication, Capital Cities / ABC., Public Relations, network programming department, November 1991.

24. Personal communication, Marcy Dolan, NBC, December 1991.

25. Minow, "How Vast the Wasteland Now?".

The Sixth Step: Neighborhoods for Learning

1. Colin Ward, *The Child in the City* (London: The Architectural Press, 1978), 86.

2. Lewis Mumford, *The Myth of the Machine: Technics and Human Development* (New York: Harcourt Brace Jovanovich, 1967); in Mary E.

Clark, "Meaningful Social Bonding as a Universal Human Need," in *Conflict: Human Needs Theory,* John W. Burton, ed. (New York: St. Martin's Press, 1990), 51.

3. Nicholas Zill, *American Children: Happy, Healthy, and Insecure* (New York: The Foundation for Child Development, 1981), 12–13, 16.

4. Carol Lawson, "Distance Makes the Heart Skip for Commuter Moms," *The New York Times,* 7 November 1991, C1.

5. Gwendolyn Wright, *Building the American Dream: A Social History of Housing in America* (New York: Pantheon, 1981), 259.

6. Carol Lawson, "Housing Plan That Forgot the Children," *The New York Times,* 21 July 1988, C1.

7. Marsha Ritzdorf, "Planning and the Intergenerational Community: Balancing the Needs of the Young and the Old in American Communities," *Journal of Urban Affairs,* vol. 9, no. 1 (1987): 84.

8. Constance Perin, *Belonging in America: Reading Between the Lines* (Madison, WI: University of Wisconsin Press, 1988), 164.

9. Zill, *American Children,* 20–21.

10. Robin C. Moore, *Childhood's Domain: Play and Place in Child Development* (London: Croom Helm, 1986), 114–26.

11. Kevin Lynch, "Spatial World of the Child"; in William Michelson et al., eds., *The Child in the City: Today and Tomorrow,* vol. 1 (Toronto: University of Toronto Press, 1979), 104.

12. Moore, *Childhood's Domain,* 50.

13. "Action Centers," *Childhood City Newsletter*, no. 23, Spring 1981, 12.

14. Joyce Rutter Kaye, "Brookie Maxwell: Walking Up Dream Street," *Upper and Lower Case: The International Journal of Type and Graphic Design,* vol. 18, no. 4, Winter 1991, 24; personal communication, Brookie Maxwell, December 1991.

15. David W. Dunlap, "The Gloom Persists on Offices," *The New York Times,* 28 July 1991, Section 10, 1.

16. Gina Gentry-Fletcher, "City's Recreation Center Redesigned for All Ages," *The Cincinnati Inquirer,* 26 August 1991, 1.

17. "Nextdoor Neighbors," *The New Yorker,* vol. 66, no. 11, 30 April 1990, 36–37.

18. Viviana Zelizer, *Pricing the Priceless Child: The Changing Social Value of Children* (New York: Basic Books, 1985), 35, 38.

19. Roger Hart, *The Changing City of Childhood: Implications for Play and Learning* (New York: City College Workshop Center, 1986), 11.

20. National Center for Education Statistics, October 1991; in *The National Education Goals Report: Building a Nation of Learners* (Washington, DC: National Education Goals Panel, 1991), 37.

21. Larry Brandwein, director, Brooklyn Public Library, letter to *The New York Times,* 2 March 1988, A22 .

22. Ann W. Lewin, "Children's Museums: A Structure for Family Learning"; in Barbara H. Butler and Marvin B. Sussman, eds., *Museum Visits and Activities for Family Life Enrichment* (Binghamton, NY: Haworth Press, Inc., 1989), 51.

23. Gordon Flagg, "The Recession and Public Libraries," *American Libraries,* vol. 22 (May 1991): 381.

24. "Budget Cut Hurts Small Library in Big Way," *Library Journal,* vol. 114 (15 May 1989): 18.

25. "Playground franchisor has big plans for strips," *Shopping Centers Today,* International Council of Shopping Centers, September 1990, 9.

26. Mark Walsh, "Minnesota Mega-Mall to Include Education Facility," *Education Week,* 9 October 1991, vol. 11, no. 6, 9.

27. Fred Rogers and Barry Head, *Mister Rogers Talks with Parents* (Pittsburgh, PA: Family Communications, Inc., 1983), 50.

The Seventh Step: Connections Across the Generations

1. Margaret Mead, *Culture and Commitment: A Study of the Generation Gap* (Garden City, New York: Natural History Press, 1970), 2.

2. John Gatto, "Our Children Are Dying in Our Schools," *New Age Journal,* September/October 1990, 62.

3. The Education Commission of the States, *State Education Leader,* vol. 10, no. 2, Summer 1991, 1.

4. "Getting Young and Old Together," *Time,* 16 April 1990, 84.

5. Edward B. Fiske with Sally Reed and R. Craig Sautter, *Smart Schools, Smart Kids* (New York: Simon and Schuster, 1991), 206.

6. James P. Comer, "Reinventing Community: A Noted Reformer's Program to Improve Education," speech, *Television and Families,* Winter 1990, 49.

7. National Commission on Children, *Beyond Rhetoric,* 343–44.

8. Hope Jensen Leichter and William E. Mitchell, *Kinship and Casework: Family Networks and Social Intervention* (New York and London: Teachers College Press, 1978), 145.

9. Patricia Edmonds, "Reunions Offer a Chance for Renewal, Celebration," *USA Today,* 13 August 1991, 5A; personal communication, Robin Johnkins, National Council of Negro Women, November 1991.

10. John Dewey, *The Public and Its Problems* in Jo Ann Boydston, ed., *John Dewey: The Later Works,* vol. 2 (Carbondale and Edwardsville: Southern Illinois University Press, 1984), 370–72; in *The Good Society* by Robert Bellah et al. (New York: Alfred A. Knopf, 1991), 263.

11. Morgan and Tucker, *Companies That Care,* 184–92.

12. Charlene Strickland, "Intergenerational Reading: Encouraging the Grandlap," *Wilson Library Bulletin,* December 1990, 164.

13. Family Friends Program, The National Council on the Aging, 1991, 2.

14. Erik H. Erikson, *The Life Cycle Completed: A Review* (New York and London: W.W. Norton and Company, 1982), 67–68.

15. Sally Newman and Julie Riess, "Older Workers in Intergenerational Child Care," a study prepared for Generations Together, University of Pittsburgh, July 1990; *Generations Together,* University of Pittsburgh, 1991.

16. Newman and Riess.

17. "University of Pittsburgh Study Affirms Elders' Role in Child Care," *The Aging Connection,* vol. xi, no. 3 (June/July 1990): 8.

18. Glenn Collins, "Wanted: Child-Care Workers, Age 55 and Up," *The New York Times*, 15 December 1987, A1.

19. Personal communication, Nancy Henkin, November 1991.

20. C. Everett Koop, M.D. and Allen V. Koop, *The Memoirs of America's Family Doctor: Koop* (New York: Random House, 1991), 14–15.

21. Suzanne MacNeille, "Catering to Older Travelers," *The New York Times*, 25 August 1991, Section 5, 9.

22. Rhoda M. Gilinsky, "Senior Volunteers Offer Helping Hands," *The New York Times*, 9 November 1986, Section 11WC, 31.

23. Ibid.

24. Rachel Carson, *The Sense of Wonder* (New York: Harper & Row, Publishers, 1965), 45.

Making it Work: A Committed Nation

1. Daniel Yankelovich, *New Rules: Searching for Self-Fulfillment in a World Turned Upside Down* (New York: Random House, Inc., 1981), 249.

2. *Kidbits: A Succinct Summary of Success by 6,* United Way of Minneapolis, Fall 1991, 1.

3. "Report of the Community Task Force," Charlotte-Mecklenburg Board of Education, May 14, 1991, meeting of the Children's Services Network, 17 October 1991.

4. Personal communication, Richard Mammen, August and November 1991.

5. Scott Armstrong, "San Francisco Voters Test Children's Issues with 'Proposition J,' " *The Christian Science Monitor,* 1 November 1991, 1-2.

6. President George Bush, "Exchange of Toasts by the President and Governor Terry Branstad," Monticello Mansion, Charlottesville, Virginia, 27 September 1989.

INDEX

185

Culture, transmission of, 109, 112
Curriculum, health, 19–20, 136
Cuyahoga Community College, 63

Darling, Sharon, 45
De Madres a Madres, 29
Delaware, 60
Denmark, 52, 104, 106
Denton, Texas, 30–31
Denver, Colo., 104
Dewey, John, 113
Ding Dong School, 84
Directory, Ready-to-Learn, 105
Discovering the First Year of Life, 88
Discovery Channel, 88
Discovery Zone, 104
Disney Channel, 88
Dobbs Ferry, N.Y., 119
Drug abuse, 16–17
Dunkirk, N.Y., 57
Durant, Will, 46
Dutchess Community College, 63

Early Childhood Family Education Program, 42–43
ECHO (Elders and Children Helping Each Other), 117
Edelman, Marian Wright, 25
Education, U.S. Department of, 36
Education Commission of the States, 111
Education Goals, 5
Education for Parenting, 20–21
Education of Young Children, National Association for the, 45, 61, 62, 63, 77, 138
Elders and Children Helping Each Other (ECHO), 117
Elliot-Pearson Department of Child Study, 63–64
Englewood, Colo., 70
Erikson, Erik, 116
Eureeka's Castle, 88

Evanston, Ill., 96
Evendale, Ohio, 97
Ewing, Stephen E., 77–78
Exploratorium, 101

Families, problems of, 3, 4, 39–41, 45, 66–67, 112
Families and Television, National Council for, 84
Family Channel, 88
Family Day Care, National Association for, 61
Family Day Care Project, 59
Family Express, 101
Family Friends, 114
Family Literacy, National Center for, 45
Family reunions, 112
Federal Communications Act, 84
Federal Government: and flextime, 72; role of, 28–29, 59, 125–126, 138
Federal Recovery Act, 50
Fetal alcohol syndrome, 16–17
Field, Tiffany, 48
Finland, 68
Flathead Indian Reservation, 53
Flextime, 65, 71–72, 139. See also Job sharing
Florida, 59–60, 63, 130
Fort Wayne, Ind., 75, 106
Fort Yates, N.D., 63
Foster Grandparents, 117–118
Framingham State College, 111
Fred Penner's Place, 88
France, 49, 52, 62
Funding, 126, 130, 136; for cultural institutions, 102; for educational television, 86; for health care, 24, 30; for preschool education, 54–56, 62; for Ready-to-Learn Clinics, 28–29; for WIC, 15, 22–23

Galveston, Texas, 28
Gardner, Howard, 38–39

187